REPORT OF ARCHAEOLOGICAL SURVEY OF THE EASTERN PART OF DISTRICT AYODHYA

(National Trust for Promotion of Knowledge, Lucknow U.P.)

VIJAY KUMAR

VANI PRAKASHAN

VANI PRAKASHAN

4695, 21-A, Daryaganj, New Delhi 110 002
Phone : +91 11 23273167 **Fax :** +91 11 23275710

India
Branch
Ashok Rajpath, Patna 800 004
Coffee House Campus, Mahatma Gandhi Marg, Allahabad 211 001, (U.P)
Mahatma Gandhi International Hindi University, Vardha 442 001, Maharashtra
www.vaniprakashan.in
vaniprakashan@gmail.com
sales@vaniprakashan.in
In Association with

ESTD.-1986
Ayodhya Research Institute
presents
Report of Archaeological Survey of the Eastern Part of District Ayodhya
by Vijay Kumar

ISBN : 978-93-88684-84-2
Gazetteer

First Edition 2019

Price : ₹ 299

Printed at Jayant Printary LLP, Mumbai-02 (India)

Vani Prakashan's signature motif is created by Artist Maqbool Fida Husain

INDEX

Introduction: District Ayodhya got its name on 6th November, 2018 from the city of same name which lies on latitude 26⁰47′18.39″ N and longitude 82⁰12′03.94″ E. Earlier the name of the district was Faizabad. Ayodhya is one of the eastern districts of Uttar Pradesh which lies between the latitude 26⁰24′26.1″ - 26⁰52′7.64″ and longitude 82⁰28′42.56″ - 82⁰33′35.09″ and its shape is fairly regular parallelogram. The river *Ghagra* forms its northern boundary and separates it from the districts *Gonda* and *Basti*. On the west lies district *Barabanki* and on the east district *Ambedkarnagar*. On the south lies district *Sultanpur*.

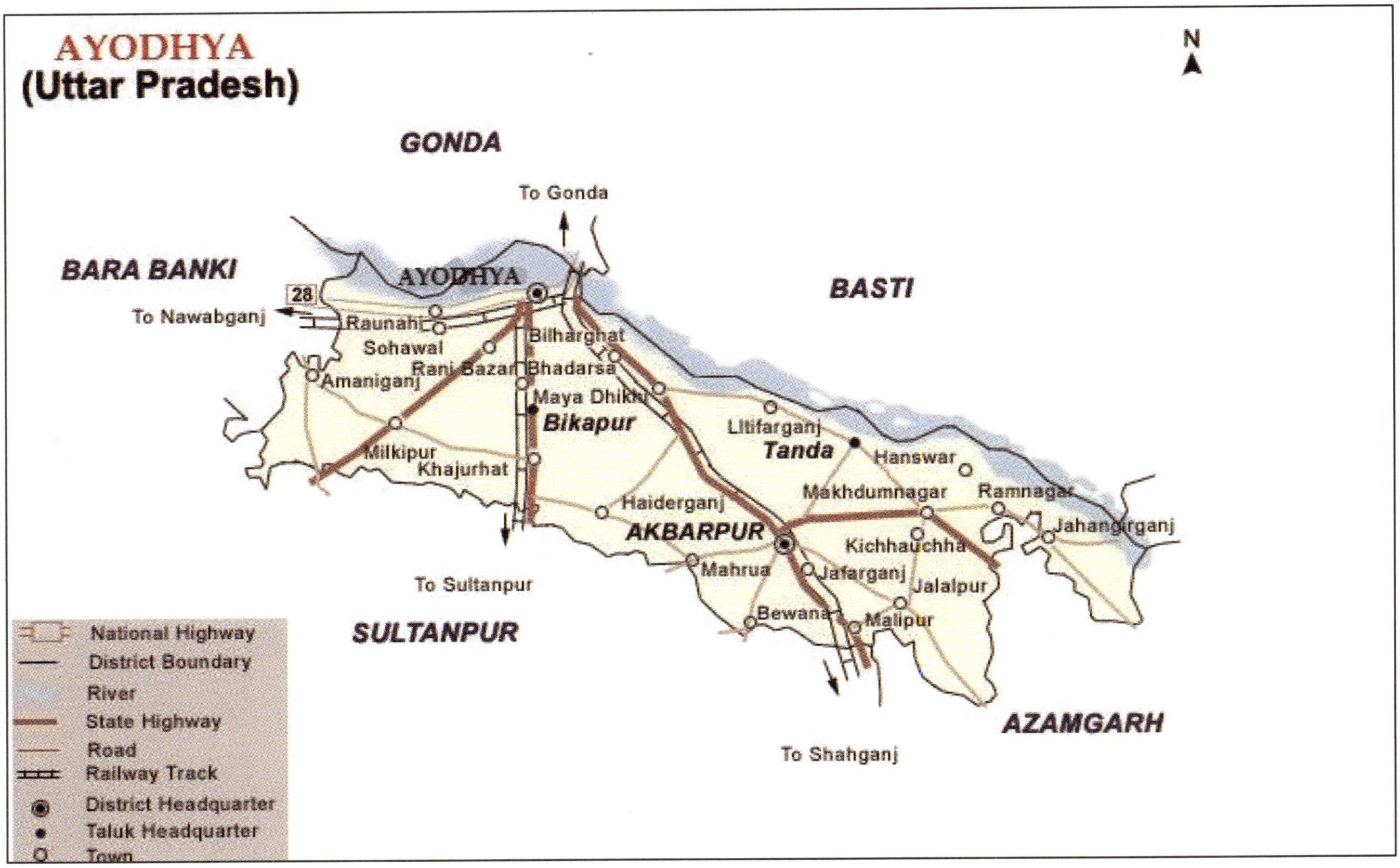

Fig. No. 01: General Map of district Ayodhya U.P. India

Demography: As per provisional reports of Census India, the district has a population of 2,468,371. This gave it a ranking of 178th in India (out of a total of 640). The district had a population density of 1,054 inhabitants per square kilometer (2,730/sq. mi). Its population growth rate over the decade 2001-2011 was 18.16%. The district had a sex ratio of 961 females for every 1000 males, and a literacy rate of 70.63%.

Area, Tehsils & Police Stations: Ayodhya is a district in the Uttar Pradesh State of India. Total area of Ayodhya is 2,341 km² including 2,266.23 km² rural area and 74.77 km² urban area. The Ayodhya district is divided in to 5 Tehsils for administrative purposes, namely 1. Bikapur, 2. Faizabad, 3. Milkipur, 4. Rudauli and 5. Sohawal. The Ayodhya district consists of 17 Police Stations, namely 1.

Ayodhya, 2. Bikapur, 3. Cantt, 4. Faizabad, 5. Gosaiganj, 6. Haiderganj, 7. Inayat Nagar, 8. Khandasa, 9. Kumarganj, 10. Maharajganj, 11. Mawai, 12. Patranga, 13. Poora Kalandar, 14. Ram Janma Bhumi, 15. Raunahi, 16. Rudauli and 16. Taroon.

History: The earliest culture found in Ayodhya and surrounding areas is OCP. This area is the part of the huge OCP complex starting from *Bara* in *Punjab* and reaching up to the straight line joining *Bahraich, Ayodhya* and *Sultanpur* along east-west axis and from foot-hill of *Himalayas* to *Vindhyan* hills and middle part of *Aravalis* (Fig. No. 02)[1]. Surprisingly this culture is uniform and it characterized by

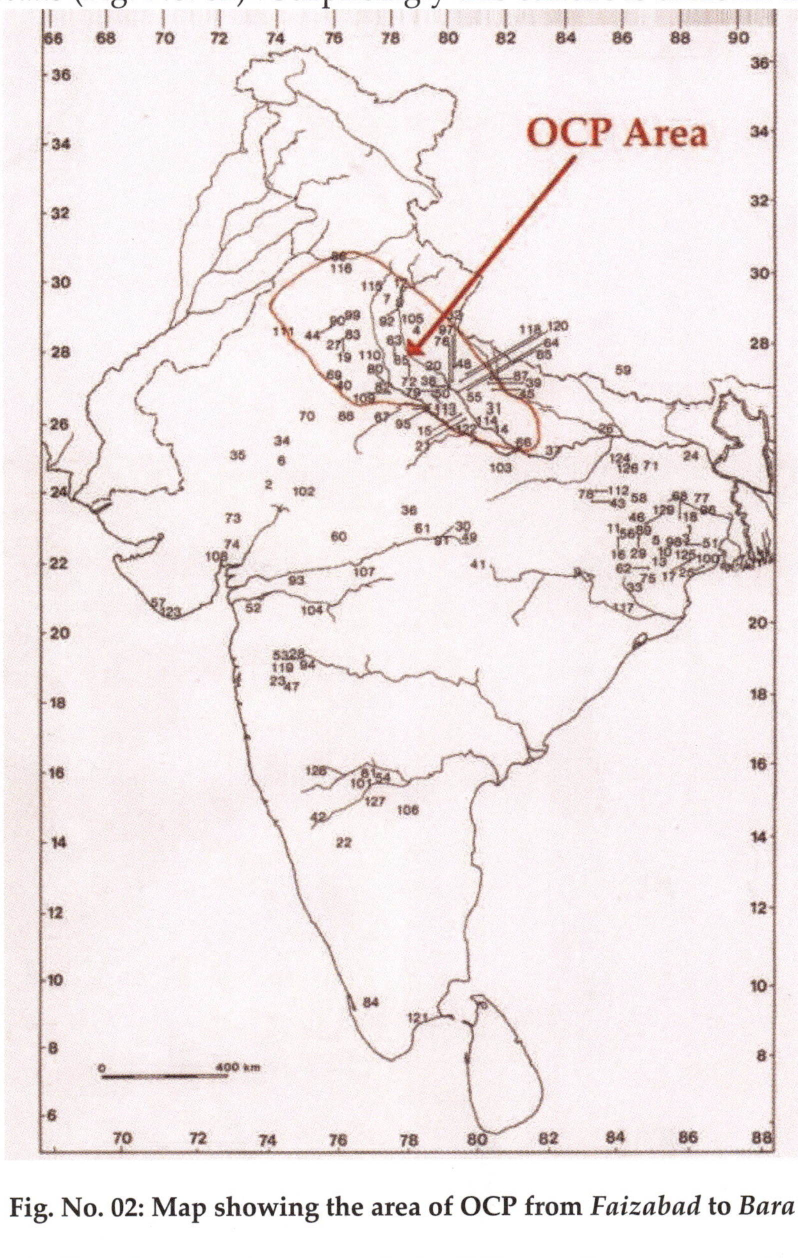

Fig. No. 02: Map showing the area of OCP from *Faizabad* to *Bara*

Copper hoard and the similar shapes of pottery. It is different from pre, early and mature *Harappans* cultures, although in upper *Ganga* doab, *Haryana, Punjab* and part of *Rajasthan*, it appears that during mature *Harappan* phase there is encroachment as gleaned from pottery shapes and other artefacts of the same period from the western part of India (Fig. No. 03)[2].

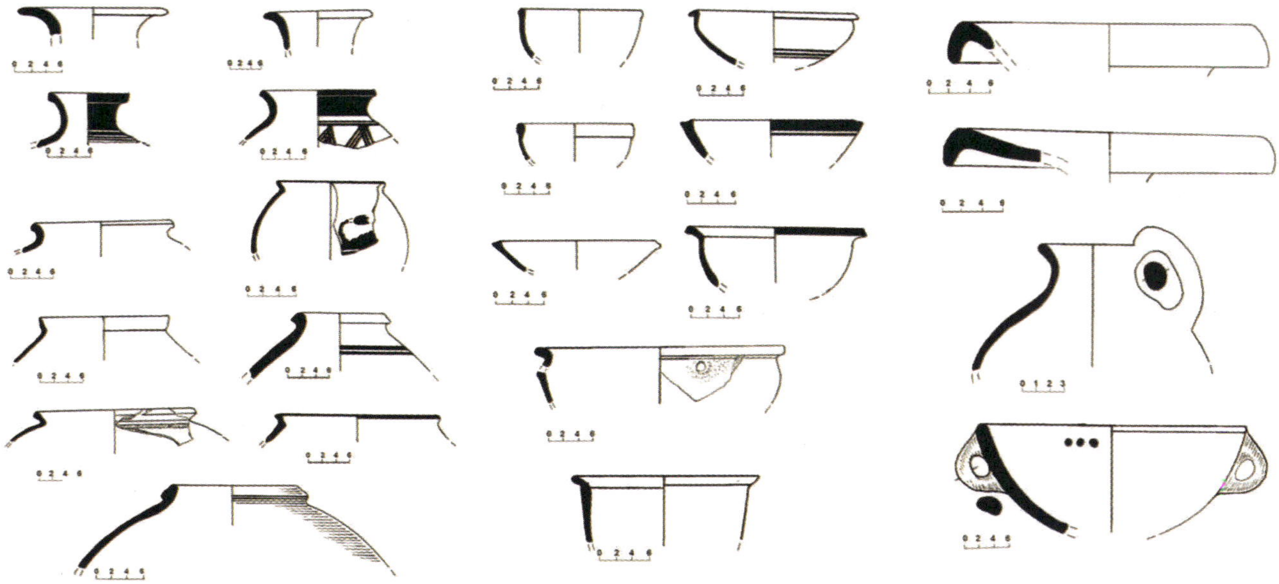

Fig. No. 03: Typical OCP pottery shapes

Some of the potteries recovered from the area in and around *Ayodhya* district are shown in the following figures (Fig. No. 04-17). Figure numbers 04-08 show the OCP pottery recovered from different places of district *Sitapur,* U.P.[3]

Fig. No. 04: OCP Pottery from village *Saraiyya Sani* p.s. *Manpur* district *Sitapur,* U.P. India

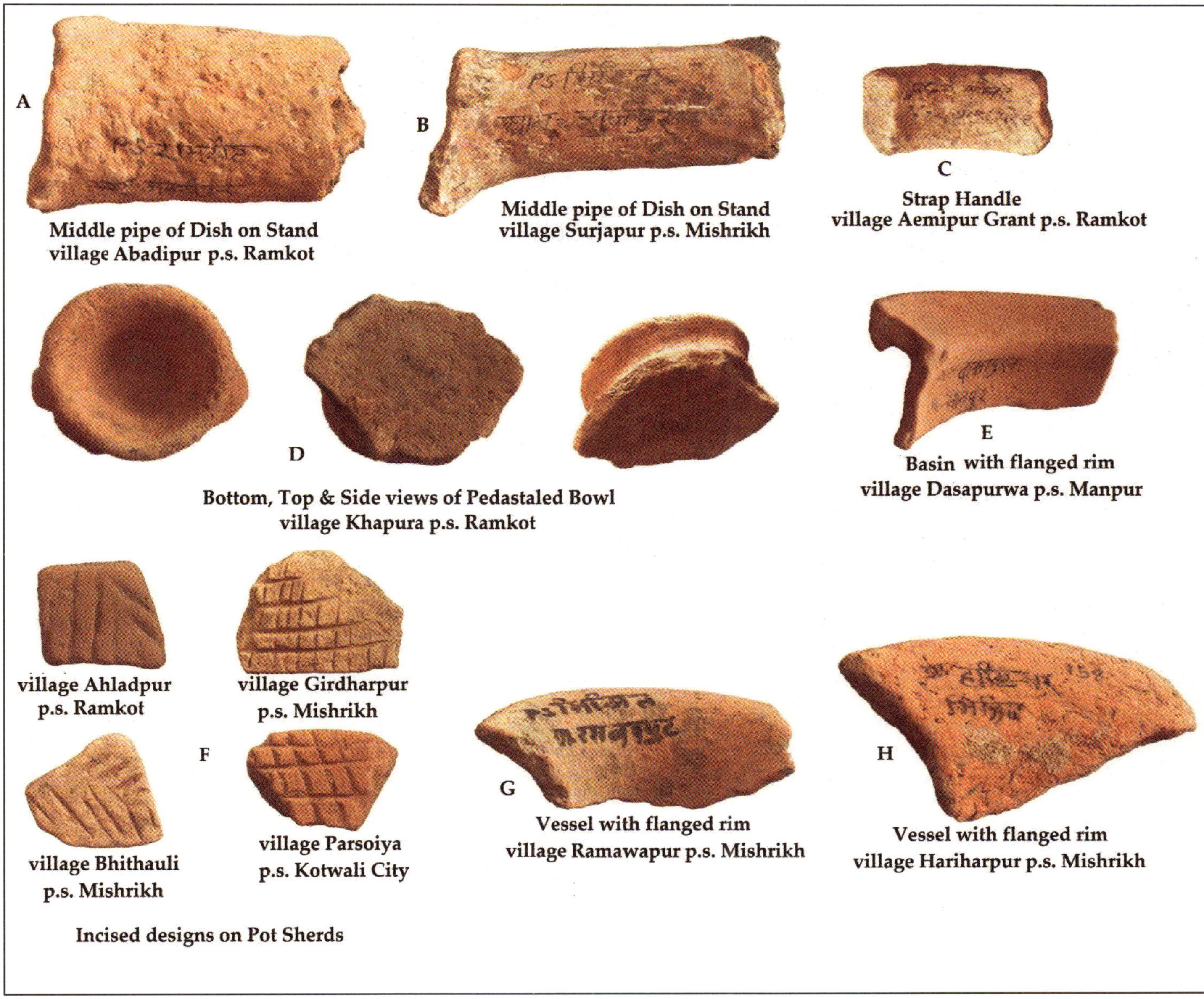

Fig. No. 05: OCP Pottery from district *Sitapur,* U.P. India

Fig. No. 06: OCP Pottery from village *Akbarganj* p.s. *Khairabad* district *Sitapur,* U.P. India

Fig. No. 07: OCP Pottery from village *Katarganj* p.s. *Maholi* district *Sitapur,* U.P. India

Fig. No. 08: OCP Pottery from village *Thakurganj* p.s. *Mishrikh* district *Sitapur,* U.P. India

Figure numbers 09-13 show the OCP pottery recovered from different places of district *Bahraich,* U.P.[4]

Fig. No. 09: OCP Pottery from village *Sarsa Tarahar* p.s. *Risiya* district *Bahraich* U.P. India

Fig. No. 10: OCP Pottery from village *Sujatpur* p.s. *Risiya* district *Bahraich* U.P. India

Fig. No. 11: OCP Pottery from village *Barai Dilasa* p.s. *Risiya* district *Bahraich* U.P. India

Fig. No. 12: OCP Pottery from village *Babhni Saida* p.s. *Risiya* district *Bahraich* U.P. India

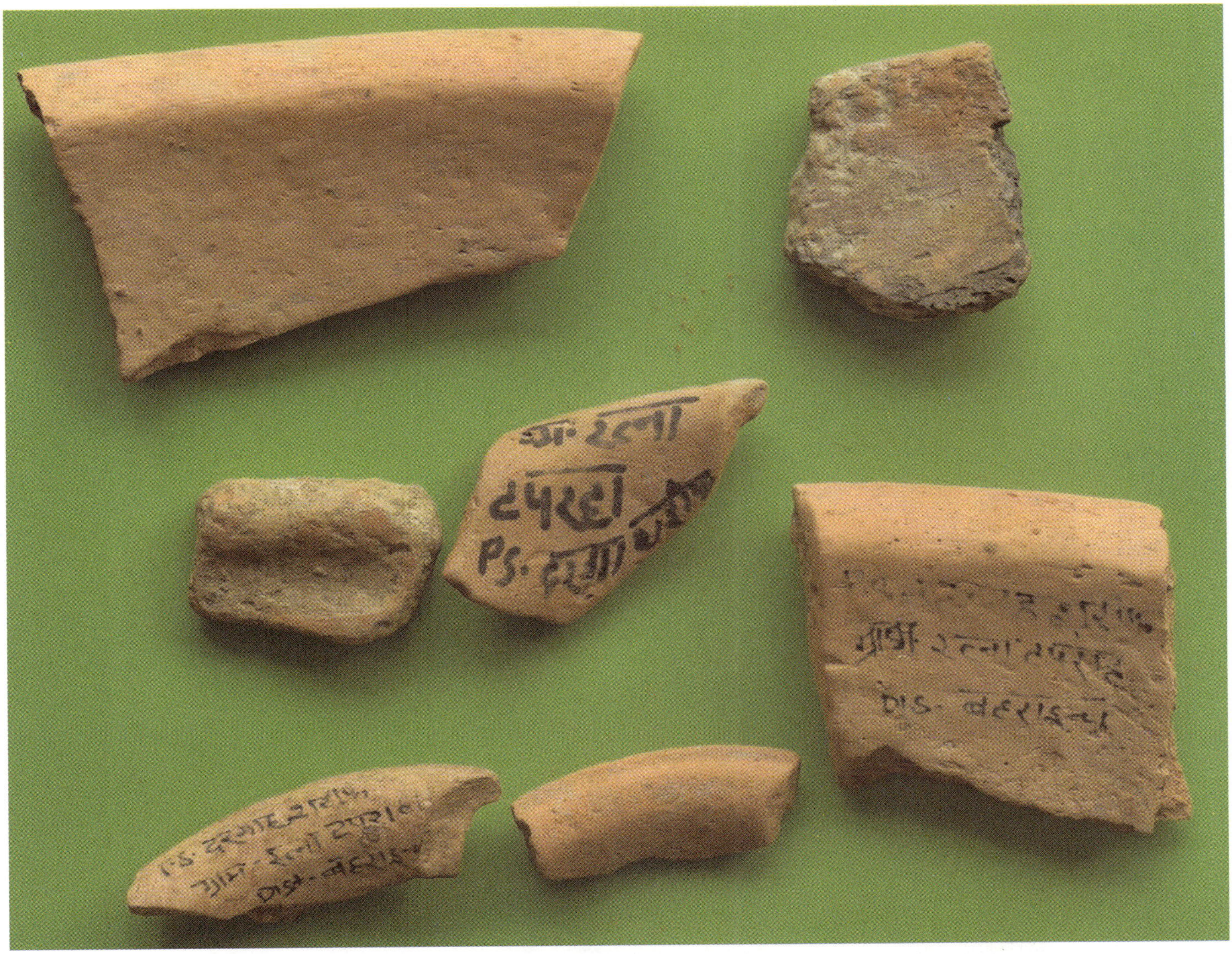

Fig. No. 13: OCP Pottery from village *Ratna Tapraha* p.s. *Dargaah Sharif* district *Bahraich* U.P. India

Figure numbers 14-17 show the OCP pottery recovered from different places of district *Sultanpur,* U.P.[5]

Fig. No. 14: OCP Pottery from village *Tajuddinpur* p.s. *Dostpur* district *Sultanpur* U.P. India

Fig. No. 15: OCP Pottery from village *Shailkha* p.s. *Dostpur* district *Sultanpur* U.P. India

Fig. No. 16: OCP Pottery from village *Viranpur* p.s. *Koorebhar* district *Sultanpur* U.P. India

Fig. No. 17: OCP Pottery from village *Dalhupur* p.s. *Jaisinghpur* district *Sultanpur* U.P. India

The Weapons, tools, artefacts and cult objects used by people belonging to OCP culture were Harpoons, flat celts, shouldered axes, chisels, antennae swords, short swords, ingots, copper rings and anthropomorphic figures. These copper antiquities have been recovered from different parts of the upper/ middle *Ganga* plains, area drained by rivers between *Yamuna* and *Sutlej* and northern portion of *Rajasthan*. These are shown in the following figures (Fig. No. 18-41). Although no copper hoard has been reported around the eastern margin of the area described here but elsewhere these weapons are found in large numbers. These artefacts can be called signature antiquities of OCP. Very few artefacts have been found from different parts of India but the major find is confined to the North and Western India. The technology used in manufacturing these weapons was typical of OCP area[6].

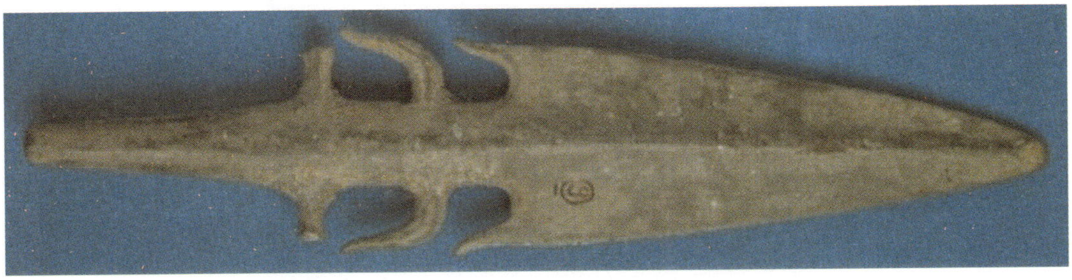

Fig. No. 18: Harpoon found from district *Shahjahanpur* U.P.

Fig. No. 19: Harpoon found from district *Shahjahanpur U.P.*

Fig. No. 20: Harpoon found from district *Shahjahanpur U.P.*

Fig. No. 21: Harpoon found from *Rohelkhand U.P.*

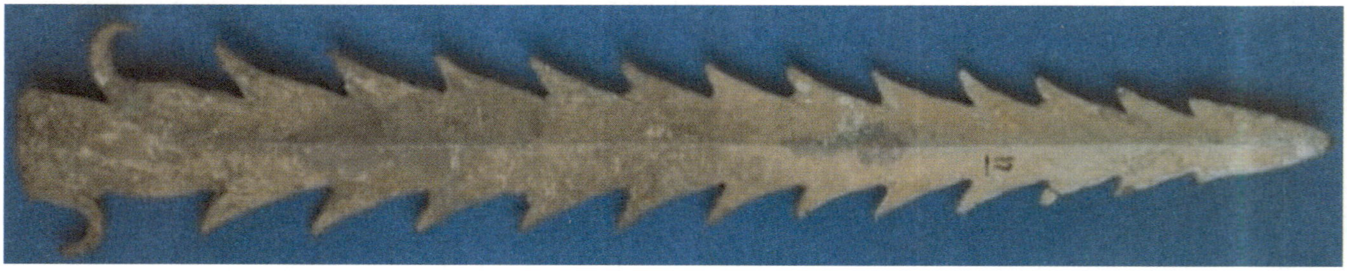

Fig. No. 22: Harpoon found from *Ahichhattra* district *Bareilly U.P.*

Fig. No. 23: Flat celt found from district *Hapur U.P.*

Fig. No. 24: Flat Axe found from district *Deeg Rajasthan*

Fig. No. 25: Shouldered Axe found from *Hastinapur* district *Meerut U.P.*

Fig. No. 26: Narrow Butt Axe found from district *Bharatpur Rajasthan*

Fig. No. 27: Lugged Shouldered Axe found from district *Bharatpur Rajasthan*

Fig. No. 28: Short Sword found from district *Shahjahanpur U.P.*

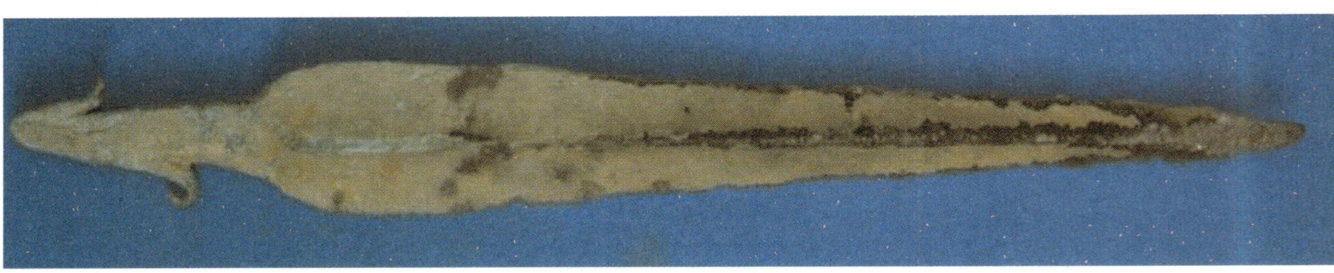

Fig. No. 29: Short Sword

Fig. No. 30: Antennae Sword found from district *Bareilly U.P.*

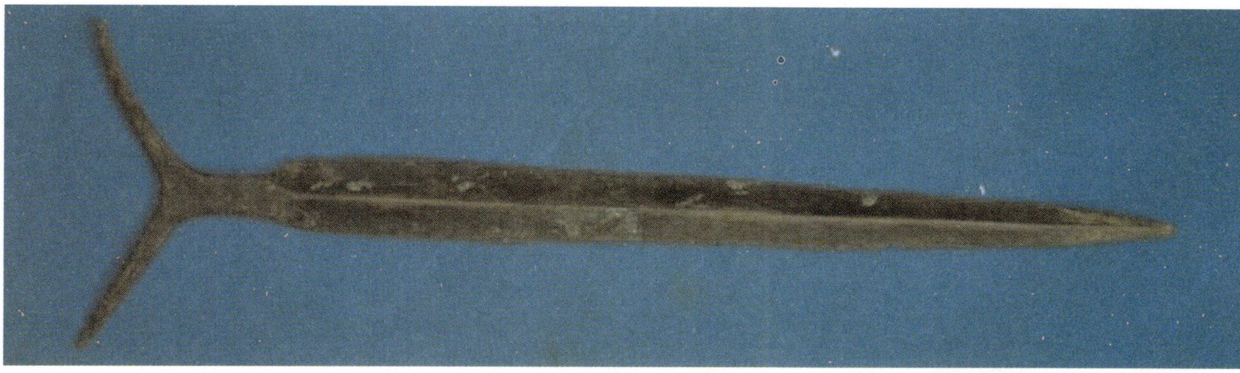

Fig. No. 31: Antennae Sword

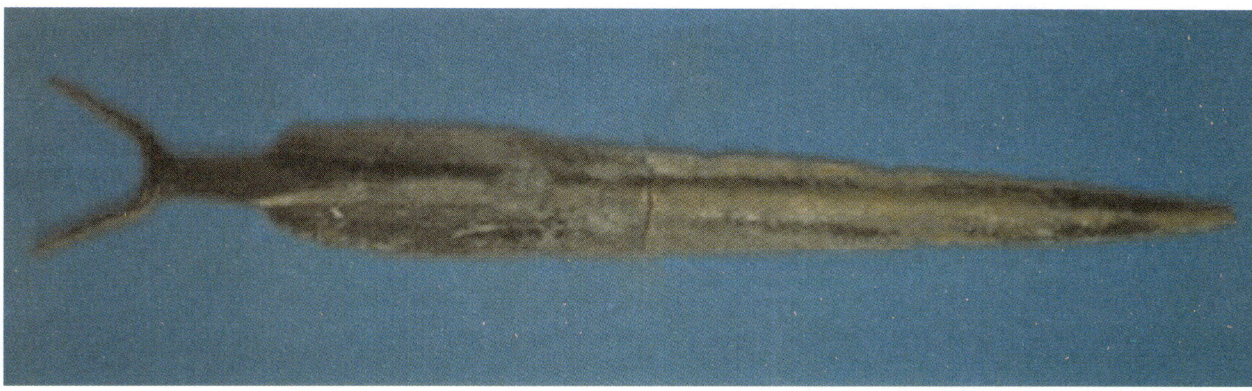

Fig. No. 32: Antennae Sword

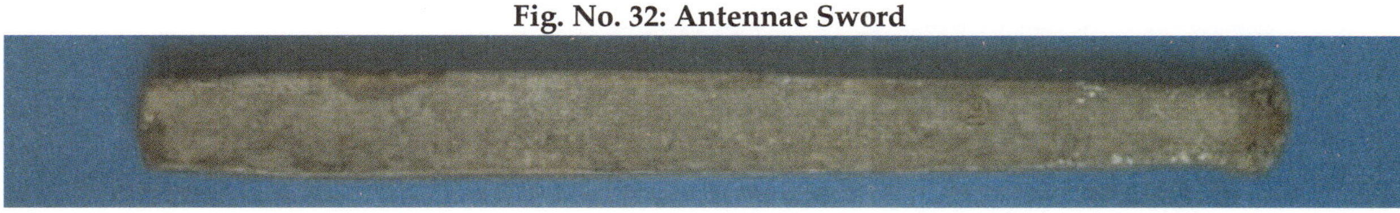

Fig. No. 33: Chisel found from district *Shahjahanpur U.P.*

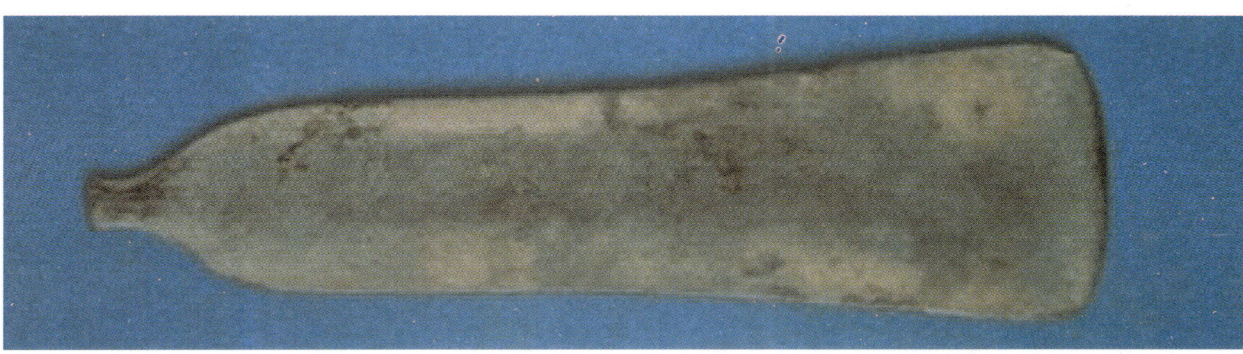

Fig. No. 34: Tanged Chisel found from district *Kaushambi U.P.*

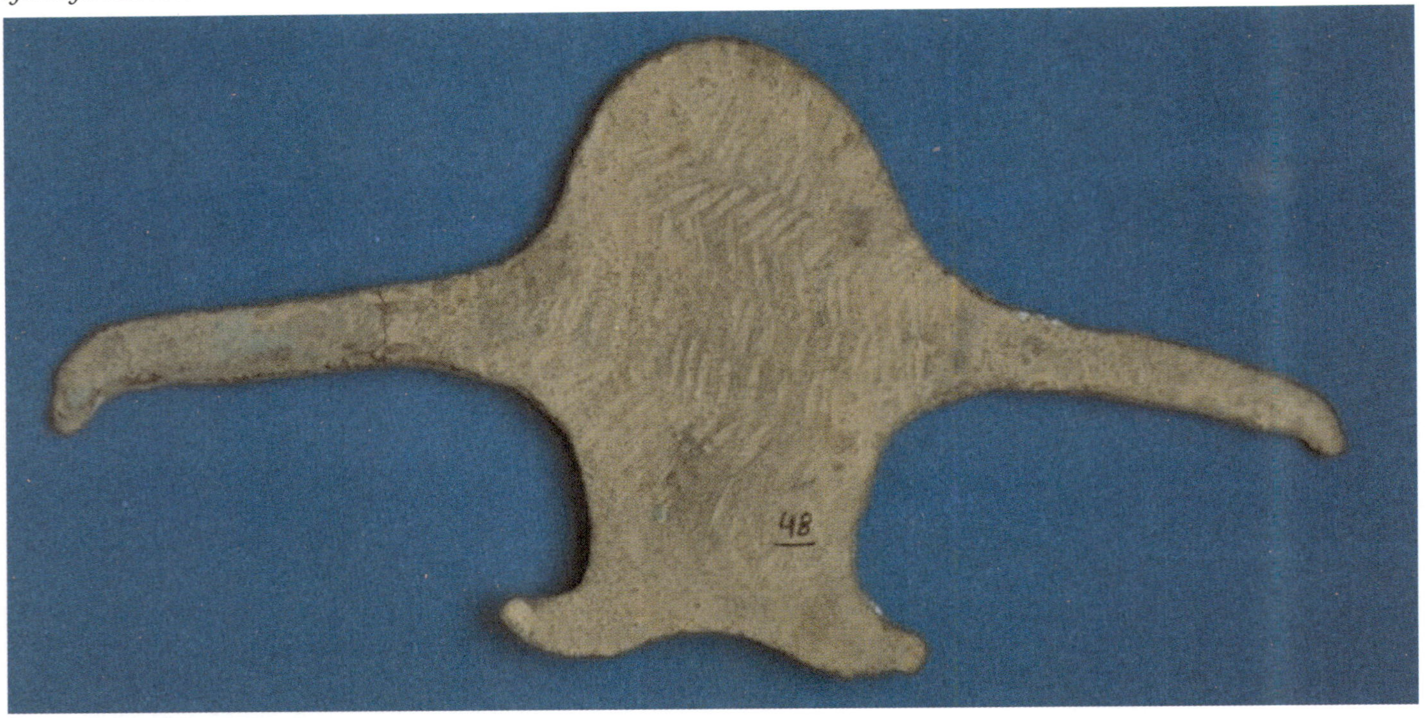

Fig. No. 35: Anthropomorphic Figure found from district *Bareilly U.P.*

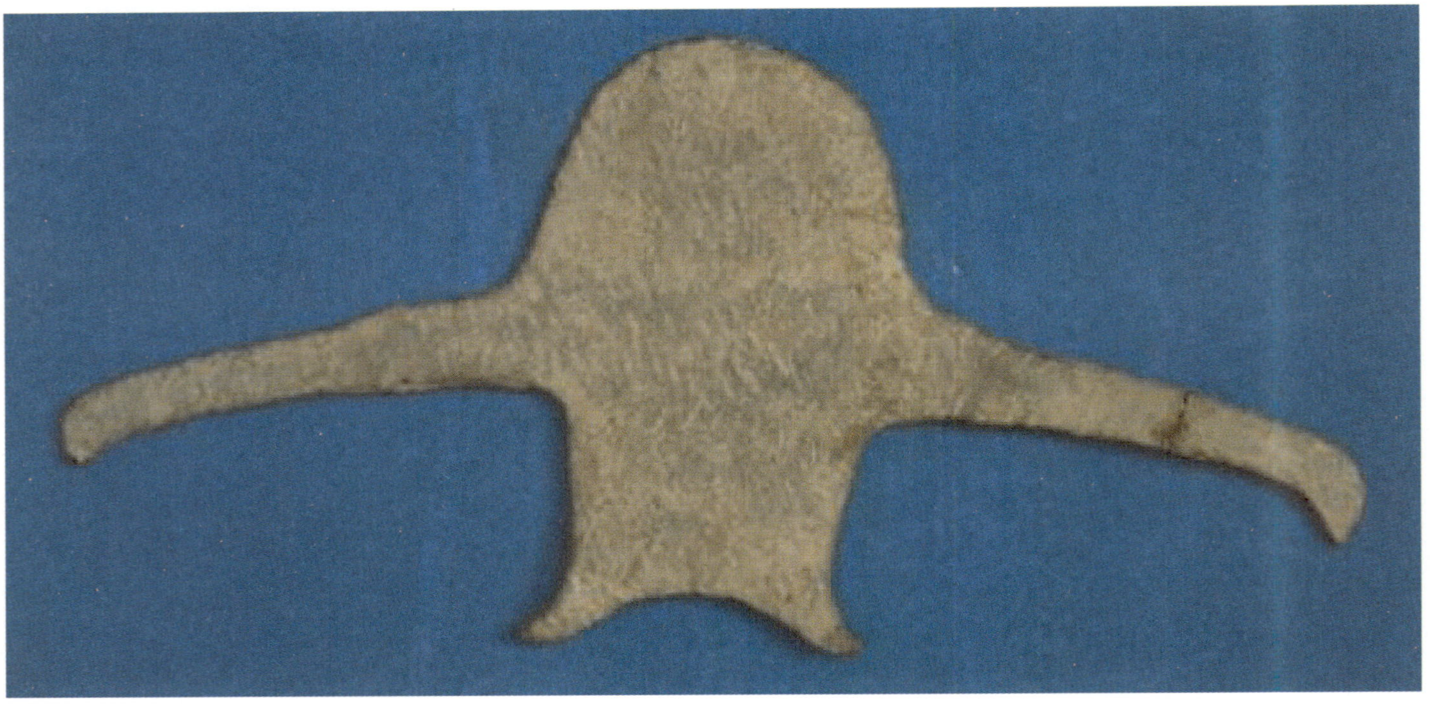

Fig. No. 36: Anthropomorphic Figure

Fig. No. 37: Anthropomorphic Figure found from district *Shahjahanpur U.P.*

Fig. No. 38: Incurved anthropomorphic figure kept in State Museum, Lucknow found from *Shivrajpur* district *Kanpur U.P.*

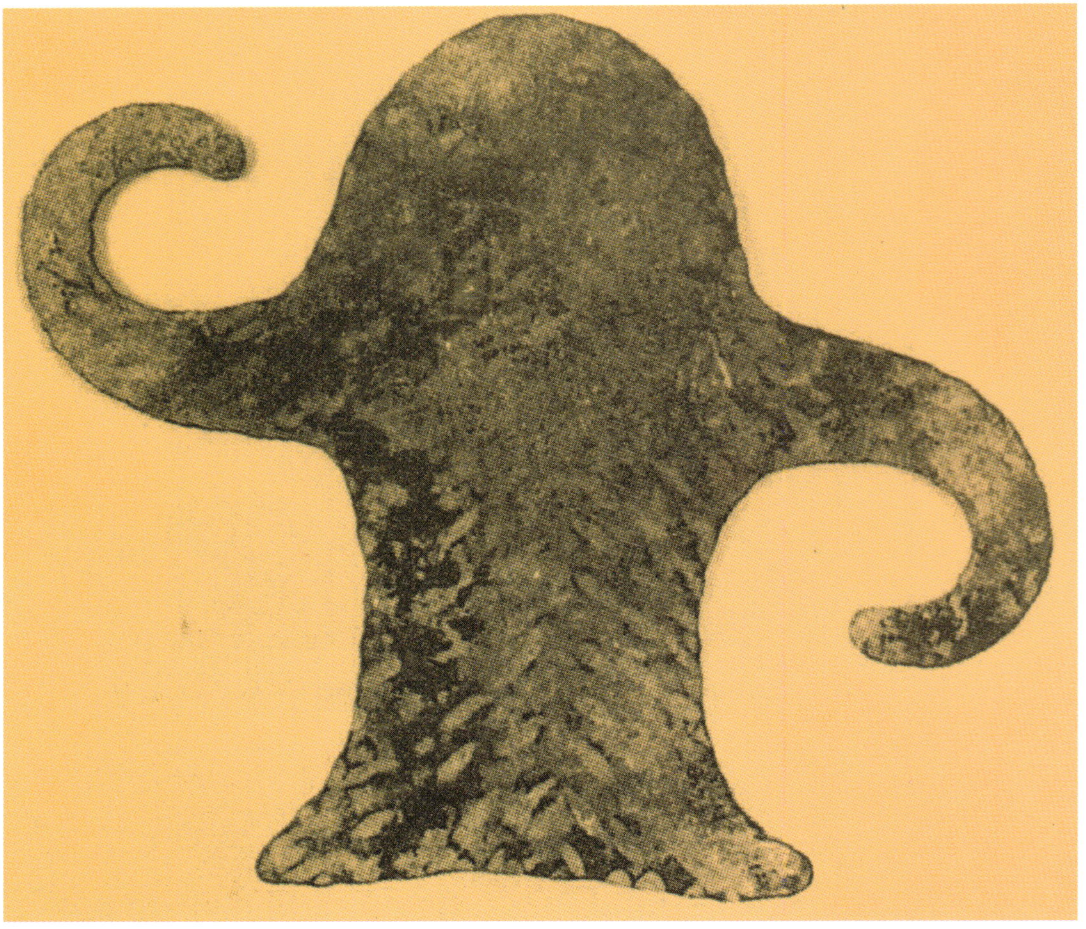

Fig. No. 39: Anthropomorphic Figure with flexed hand kept in National Museum found from *Madarpur U.P.*

Fig. No. 40: Thick Solid Ring found from district *Amroha U.P.*

Fig. No. 41: Ingot found from district *Hapur U.P.*

A large number of OCP burials were found at *Sanauli* district *Baghpat U.P.* This is the only OCP site where burials have been excavated thoroughly. It appears that many types of burials were practiced at this place. All graves had north-west, south-east orientation with head placed in the north and legs in the south (Fig. No. 42). Majority of the burials (Fifty-two in number) were extended burials. Thirty-five were symbolic secondary burials yielding fragmentary bones and Twenty-nine burials did not yield human bones but only grave goods. Pottery was placed near the head, the vessel of different shapes and sizes were arranged in odd numbers namely three, five, seven, nine, eleven and so on. The maximum number noted in the case of triple burial was Twenty-one[7].

Fig. No. 42: Triple Burial

The main pottery types placed in the grave were bowls, decanters, vases and dish on stands. The dish on stand was placed mostly below the hip or head of the dead man. Only in few instances, it was found placed close to the feet. Food grains & meat were found placed on dish on stand. In another burial, a horse chariot was buried with the elaborately carved four legged wooden coffin containing the corpse[8] (Fig. No. 43).

Fig. No. 43: ***S. K. Manjul*** **at the excavation site,** ***Sinauli Baghpat*** **U.P. (Courtesy: Archaeological Survey of India)**

After this, BRW culture makes its appearance in the district which came from eastern-most part of U.P. (it extends further east into state of Bihar) where it evolved from the Neolithic corded ware tradition. After this comes BSW in this district. Then NBP appears here. According to literary traditions, *Ikshvaku,* the son of *Vaivasvata Manu* and the first king of solar line founded this city. Jain literary narrative makes Ayodhya the capital of *Rishabhanatha,* the first *Tirthankara* who predated even *Ikshvaku*, according to literary traditions. *Ikshvaku* was succeeded by his son *Vikukshi*. Another king of this line name *Shravasta* founded the city of *Shravasti* which in later time became the capital of *Uttar Kosala*. A few generations later came the great *Mandhata* who was a universal monarch. *Purukutsa,* the son of *Mandhata,* defeated the *Gandharvas* and married a *Naga* princess and his grandson *Anaranya,* was killed in a battle about 15 miles from Ayodhya. The 31st king *Harishchandra,* well known as the lover of truth, was a mighty ruler who performed the *Rajasuya* sacrifice. The 37th king *Bahu,* in whose time the *Kosala* power suffered a great reverse at the hands of his enemies, was forced to abdicate. His posthumous son, *Sagar,* vanquished the *Haihayas* and the *Tala janghas*. He performed the horse sacrifice. *Jain* tradition makes *Ajitanatha,* a contemporary of *Sagar*. *Sagar's* great grandson, *Bhagiratha,* is reputed to have brought the *Ganga* to earth by virtue of his penances. *Bhagiratha* great grandson, *Ambarisha* in whose reign Ayodhya again rose to prominence, was a great donor and a repute devotee of *Vishnu*. His grandson *Rituparna,* was a contemporary of the celebrated *Vidarbha* monarch. *Nala* to whom, he taught the secrets of the art of throwing the dice and from whom he acquired the science of training horses. *Rituparna's* grandson was *Sudasa* who is often identified with the *vedic Sudasa* of the *Dasarajna* war. It was in the time of his successor, *Kalmashpada* and the kings that followed that the kingdom of Ayodhya seemed to have suffered reverses. The result was that *Kalmashpada's* grandson *Mulaka* had to be brought up secretly, thus becoming the only source through whom the royal family of *Kosala* was enabled to continue. There was, however, a bifurcation in the line for some six or seven generations, the two stream being united in a single monarchy under *Khatvanga,* also known as *Dilipa.* Some scholars think that it was under this great king and his immediate descendants that this region acquired the name of *Kosala.* His son was the great *Raghu* after whom the family came to be called *Raghuvansha.* He is credited with conquering the whole earth and performing the *Visvajit* sacrifice. His son *Aja* was married to the *Vidarbha* princess *Indumati,* the mother of *Dasharatha* who was powerful enough to lead his campaigns far and wide and to perform the horse sacrifice at Ayodhya. It was in *Ramachandra,* the eldest son of *Dasharatha,* that the glory of *Kosala* royal dynasty reached its culmination. *Kosala* emerges into great prominence in this period, its princes carrying *Aryan* civilization as far as Ceylon. The story of this epoch has been immortalized by *Valmiki* and immensely popularized by the great mass of subsequent literature of *Rama.*

After *Rama,* the extensive *Kosala* Empire was divided among his sons and three brothers. In *Kosala,* itself *Rama's* elder son *Kusha* ascended the throne of *Ayodhya* and the younger son *Lava* became the ruler of the northern part of the kingdom with its capital of *Shravasti. Kusha* soon transferred his capital to *Kushasthali* which he himself had founded at the foot of the *Vindhyas* range. Thus Ayodhya became deserted and although later *Kusha* tried to restore it, the city could not regain its old position.

Hiranyabha Kausalya, the 81st king in the line and the 17th in descent from *Kusha,* was a great monarch who is said to have been a disciple of *Jaimini* and to have taught the science of *Yoga* to *Yajnavalkya.*

In the 93rd generation from *Ikshvaku* and the 30th from *Rama* was *Brihadbala,* the last famous king of the *Ikshvaku* dynasty of Ayodhya. He was killed in *Mahabharata* war. Five generations later, a king of the name of *Divakara* was ruling at Ayodhya and the last known king of the line was *Sumitra* in whose reign the advent of *Kaliyuga* took place and the family came to an end.

It may be noted here that the list of 31st post *Mahabharata* kings includes the names of *Sakya, Suddodhana, Siddhartha* and *Rahul,* immediately before *Prasenjit.* It is known from *Buddhist* sources that a *Prasenjit* son of *Mahakosala* was a contemporary of the *Buddha.* Thus though the *puranic* lists do contain names of some kings and princes who actually lived, it is not easy to prove the existence of all the kings of these *puranic* chronicles[9].

According to Buddhist accounts, there was continued rivalry for supremacy between the neighboring kingdoms of *Kashi* and *Kosala.* By the beginning of the 6th century B.C., the kingdom of *Kashi* was eventually annexed by the *Kosala* king *Mahakosala* who has been mentioned as the sovereign of both *Kashi* and *Kosala.*

The kingdom of *Kosala* at this time was probably bounded by the *Sadanira* on the east, *Panchala* on the west, *Sarpika* or *Syandika* on the south and the Nepal hills on the north. It was divided into north *Kosala* and South *Kosala* by the river *Sarayu. Shravasti* was the capital of the former and *Kushavati* that of the latter. *Saketa* also finds mention as a capital city and is often taken to be identical with Ayodhya, but the separate mention of both as existing in Buddha's time precludes that supposition. It is, however, certain that in this period Ayodhya had sunk into insignificance, whereas *Saketa* and *Shravasti* figured among the six great cities of India.

The conquest of *Kashi* made *Kosala* a powerful state. During the reign of *Mahakosala's* son *Prasenjit,* the kingdom attained even greater prosperity and enjoyed precedence as the premier state of upper India. But towards the end of his reign it had begun to be eclipsed by the growing power of *Magadha* under *Ajatashatru,* the son and successor of the king *Bimbisara* who had been an intimate ally of *Prasenjit.*

To this period belong the two great personalities, *Gautam Buddha* and the *Tirthankara Mahavira.* Both are said to have enjoyed the patronage of *Prasenjit* in whose reign *Kosala* became an important center of their proselytizing activities[10].

In the 4th century B.C. the *Nanda* kings occupied the imperial throne of *Magadha* and *Kosala.* Ayodhya was an integral part of their dominion. The *Kathasaritsagara* also refers the existence of the camp of the *Nanda* king in Ayodhya. About the beginning of the last quarter of the 4th century B.C., the *Mauryas* surperseded the *Nandas.* In circa 184 B.C. *Pushyamitra,* the *Brahmana* general of the last *Maurya* king assassinated his master and captured the throne thus founding the *Sungas* dynasty which lasted till 75 B.C. There is no doubt that Ayodhya was included in the dominions of the *Sungas* and was probably a vice royalty. Although it was then governed from far off capital, *Pataliputra,* it was famous and prosperous enough to attract the adventurous Greek invaders. The Greek invasion is alluded to by the grammarian *Patanjali* in terms which imply that this event occurred during his lifetime and his allusion is corroborated by the *Yugapurana* which states that the viciously valiant Greeks overran *Saketa* or *Avadh, Panchala* and *Mathura* and reached *Pataliputra.* Opinion, however, is divided who was the invader. Some say it was Demetrius and others that it was Menander[11].

An inscription discovered at Ayodhya reads: "*Dharmarajna Dhana,* the son of *Kaushika* and the sixth from *Senapati Pushyamitra,* the lord of *Kosala,* who had performed two horse sacrifices, built a mansion for his father *Phalgudeva".* It is entirely in Sanskrit and is one of the earliest known inscriptions in this language.

The *Senapati Pushyamitra,* mentioned in the inscription seems to be identical with the founder of the *Sunga* dynasty and *Dhanadeva,* the author of this record appears to have been some prince sixth in descent from him probably on the maternal side. *Dhanadeva* and his inscription can be placed somewhere in the later part of the 1st century B.C. This prince seems to have been closely associated with the *Kosala* branch of the *Sungas* which was founded by *Muladeva* who according to the poet *Bana,* killed *Sumitra* in circa 123 B.C. and who is in all probability identical with the king of that name whose coins have been found near about Ayodhya.

In 1865, a hoard of copper coins was discovered in the vicinity of Ayodhya. These coins have been divided into three classes and are, with the exceptions of one class presumably the currency of a wider area, the kingdom of *Kosala* of which Ayodhya was the capital. The first class consists of a few rare castes pieces of which three types are known. It has been suggested that these are local coins of the city as distinct from dynamic coins. They bear no inscription and probably belong to the third century B.C. The second includes square coins which are obviously cast. They show no trace of foreign influence in their style and type. The devices are, on the obverse, a bull or elephant before an elaborate symbol not always distinct end, on the reverse, a group of five or six symbols including a tree-in-railing, the *swastika,* a group of four *nandipadas,* a small Ujjain symbol, a river or snake and another peculiar symbol. The evidence of this type of coins shows that a dynasty ruled in Ayodhya about the second and first centuries B.C. The names of rulers inscribed on these coins are: *Muladeva, Vayudeva, Vishakhadeva, Dhanadeva, Shivadatta* and *Nardatta*. Though the actual sequence of these rulers is not known in all probability they belong to the same dynasty the *Kosala* branch of the *Sungas* and must have enjoyed a position little short of independence.

The *Sungas* line of Ayodhya had certainly become extinct with the advent of the *Kushanas* into whose hand *Kosala* passed in the 1st century A.D. and who ruled over it for a century or so. Tibetan and Chinese writings contain the traditions of *Kanishka's* conflict with the kings of *Saketa* and *Pataliputra* and of their being subdued by him. This victory brought to him the famous poet and theologian, *Ashvaghosha* author of *Buddhacharita* and *Saundarananda,* who was originally a learned *Brahmana* of *Saketa* and had become a convert of *Buddhism*.

The third class belongs to a later dynasty and the coins are round pieces, struck from dies and usually bearing on the obverse the device of a bull facing an upright standard or spear and on the reverse a bird and a palm tree with a river and sometimes a framed *nandipada* also. The names of rulers supplied by this series are: *Satyamitra, Ayumitra, Sanghamitra, Vijayamitra, Kumudasena, Ajavarman* and *Devami-tra.* The actual sequence of these rulers is not known but there is little doubt that they belong to a single dynasty and were probably feudatories of the *Kushanas.* It appears that their rule lasted till the rise of the *Guptas*[12].

Chandragupta I was the great real founder of the kingdom which he extended up to *Saketa* and *Prayag.* If the spurious *Gaya* copper plate inscription is to be believed, his son and successor, the great conqueror *Samudragupta* had a *jayaskandhavara* in Ayodhya. The *Vayupurana* also mentions that *Saketa* was included in the domains of the *Guptas*.

According to the tradition, the credit for the restoration of Ayodhya goes to king *Vikramaditya* of *Ujjain,* who is usually identified with *Chandragupta II Vikramaditya* (379-413 A.D.), the son and successor of *Samudragupta.* There is reason to believe that in the 5th century A.D. Ayodhya rather than *Pataliputra* was the premier city of the *Gupta* Empire.

The Chinese pilgrim Fa-hien who travelled in India for more than ten years (400-411 A.D.) during the reign of *Chandragupta II,* passed through Avadh and visited the city of *Shachi* where he found that the Buddhists and the Brahmans were not on good terms. Here he saw a *stupa* where the four *Buddhas* had walked and sat, and also the tree that had sprouted from the toothbrush stick thrown away by the Buddha. While some scholars have identified this *Sha-chi* of Fa-hien with the *Sageda* of Ptolemy's and consequently with our *Saketa,* others have questioned this identifications. A view is held that Ayodhya continued to occupy an important position even after *Skandagupta* and that the later rulers of the dynasty had a capital of Ayodhya probably till the rise of the *Maukharis*.

With the decline of the *Guptas* in the 6th century A.D. Ayodhya also began gradually to become desolate. At this time a new dynasty that of the *Maukharis* with its capital at *Kannauj,* assumed an important position on the political map of northern India and this kingdom included Avadh. A large hoard of *Maukhari* coins was discovered in village *Bhitaura* (*pargana Mangalsi, tehsil Faizabad*) and some were found by Rivett Carnac in Ayodhya itself. Many of these coins were found to be associated with those of *Shiladitya-Pratapshila* whom Sir Richard Burn identifies with *Harsha Vardhana* (606-47 A.D.) into whose hands the dominions of the *Maukharis* had passed. If this is correct, it would be a direct proof that Ayodhya was under the rule of *Harsha*.

During his reign the famous Chinese pilgrim Hiuen Tsang (630-644 A.D.) passed through Avadh. Travelling from *Kannauj* and crossing the *Ganga* to the south, he reached the *O-yu-to* country. The capital of this country, which was about a mile to the south of the river has generally been identified with Ayodhya although on account of difficulties of direction and distance, Cunningham proposed a different site for Hiuen Tsang's O-yu-to.

According to Hiuen Tsang, this region yielded good crops, was luxuriant in fruits and flowers and had a genial climate. The people had agreeable ways, were found of good deeds and were devoted to practical learning. Here, there were about 100 Buddhist monasteries, more than 3000 *Mahayani* and *Hinayani* monks and only ten *deva* temples, the non-Buddhists being but few in number. Then the pilgrim goes on to give an account of the Buddhist scholars, *Asanga* and *Vasubandhu* and of the Buddhist monuments of the place but is silent about its government.

Soon after *Harsha's* death, his empire fell to pieces and about half a century of darkness and anarchy ensued which were dispelled by the emergences of the great *Yashovarmana* of *Kannauj*. He seems to have launched a tour of victory, described by his court poet *Vakpatiraja* in his epic *Gaudavaha*. It is said that after conquering the south, he marched to the site of Ayodhya, the city of *Harishchandra* and received the submission of the people living in the *Mandara* Mountains. Thus in the 8th century too, Ayodhya had not lost its importance and was included in the empire of *Kannauj*. Vincent Smith however thinks that it is some other Ayodhya further north. Nothing definite is known about *Yashovarmana's* immediate successors[13].

In the beginning of the 9th century A.D., the *Gurjara Pratihara* king, *Nagabhatta II,* over threw the Ayudhas who were then ruling in *Kannauj* and made this city the capital of his growing empire rose to its greatest height in the reign of the famous *Mihir Bhoja* (836-885 A.D.). The whole of Avadh was evidently under his rule and the records of his successor, *Mahendrapala I* (885-908 A.D.) have also been found here. However, from the times of *Mahipala* (912-944 A.D.), the power of *Kannauj* began to decline and different parts of the empire gradually began to fall away.

Avadh, too, was divided into a number of small chieftain ships including that of *Srivastavas* of Ayodhya who originally belonged to the trans-Ghaghra regions. They are said to have crossed the river *Sarayu* under the leader *Trilokachandra* and to have occupied Ayodhya and founded this kingdom in 918 A.D. All of them had ultimately to yield to the newly growing power of the *Gahadavalas* of *Kannauj*.

Some of the records of the *Gahadwal* dynasty assert the proud claim that *Chandradeva* (1085-1100 A.D.), the virtual founder of the *Gahadwal* kingdom of *Kannauj,* wad the protector of the holy places of *Kashi, Kushika, Uttarkosala* and *Indraprastha,* after he had obtained them, *Uttar Kosala* being the old name of the country round about Ayodhya. *Chandradeva* appears to have begun his career modestly in his ancestral domain of *Varanasi-Ayodhya, Jayachandra* (1170-9 A.D.), the last important ruler of the dynasty granted in *Vikrama Samvat 1243* (1186 A.D.), the village of *Komali* near Ayodhya to *Alanga,* a *Brahman* of the *Bhardwaj Gotra* and a resident of that village. This shows that his kingdom included Ayodhya. In 1194 A.D., *Jayachandra* was killed in the battle of *Chandawar* fighting against the invading army of *Shihab-ud-din Ghori*. Soon after his death *Kannauj* was occupied by the Turks.

Local traditions state that for centuries Ayodhya was a wilderness and that the greater part of Avadh was occupied by the *Bhars*. No definite evidence is available about the origin and early history of these people. Formerly it was believed that *Dalki* and *Malki,* who commanded the fort of *Kalinjar,* were *Bhar* princes but this theory did not hold ground for long and Cunningham identified them with *Dalkeshvara* and *Malkeshvara,* the two *Baghel Rajas.* The evidence of an extensive *Bhar* kingdom in the district can be gleaned only for the *dihs* popularly ascribed to the *Bhars* and found extant in a number of villages of the district. There is no legend regarding any particular capital of the *Bhars* but it has been suggested that this country was under the sway of the *Bhar* chieftains who resided at *Kusavantpur* or *Kusapur,* the old name of *Sultanpur.* A few *Bhars* are still found in the village *Mudna* and *Bhitaura* of *tehsil Faizabad.*

The overthrow of the *Bhars* was followed by colonization of the whole country by *Rajput* chieftains ruled over by clans. It appears that various *Muslims* rulers coming from west settled different families of *Rajput* who were loyal to them and completely reduced the old ruling class.

In the western *parganas* colonies were formed by the *Chauhans* from *Mainpuri,* the Bisens from *Majhauli* and the *Bais* from *Baiswara.* According to the brahmanical legend about their origin, the *Chauhans* had sprung from the sacred fire pit kindled by the *Brahmanas,* around which the priests had assembled and prayed to *Mahadeva.* Another account derives the name of the clan from *Chaturbahu,* the first king of the tribe. Cunningham shows from inscriptions that even as late as the time of *Prithviraja,* the *Chauhans* did not claim to have sprung from fire but were content to be considered descendants of sage *Bhrigu.* Whatever their real origin may have, they came to this district from *Mainpuri* from where all the Avadh members of this clan claim to have sprung.

The *Bisens* claim descent from one *Mayura Bhatta* who is also said to have been a descendant of *Jamadagni Rishi* of the race of *Bhrigu.* Local traditions are very vague about this ancestor. Some say he came from *Hastinapur* and was the son of *Ashvaththama* while others hold he was an emigrant from *Maharashtra.* By one of his three wives, he is said to have had a son named *Biswa* or *Bissusena* who was the ancestor of the *Bisen.* The *Bais* claim descent from *Salivahana,* the mythical son of snakes who conquered *Raja Vikramaditya* of *Ujjain.*

The *Bachhagotis* in the south and center of the district are said to have been *Chauhans* originally. The traditions with regard to *Bariar Singh,* the founder of the clan, are so numerous and consistent that he may be assumed to have been a historical figure. The *Surajbansis* of *Haveli Avadh* and *Amsin* appear to have come at a much later date. They claim to be the representatives of the famous solar race of Ayodhya. The *Gargabansis* of *Haveli Avadh* and *Paebhimaratha* claim to be the descendants of the *Garga Rishi* who was the father of *Sini* from whom according to the *Vishnu purana,* the *Gargyas* and *Sainyas,* '*Brahmins* of *Kshatriya* race', had sprung. In Faizabad, the *Gargabansis* claim that their ancestor, the *rishi* was summoned from *Kannauj* by *Raja Dashratha* to assist him in performing the horse sacrifice others say that he had been sent for from *Kekaidesha* by *Vikramaditya* on his restoration of Ayodhya.

The *Palwars* in the east of the district state that they were originally *Somabansis* from *Pali* but whether they are a branch of the *Pratapgarh* family or of that *Pali* in *Hardoi,* is uncertain. According to the local tradition, one *Prithviraj Somabanshi* known also as *Mardeo* or *Bhardeo,* came from the village of *Pali* in 1248 A.D. and took up his residence in village *Rannupur* where he accepted service under the *Bhars.* He gave up the appellation *Somabanshi* and instead adopted that of *Palwar,* derived from his native place *Pali.* According to another version, the founder of the sept was one *Patraja* of the *Somabanshi* line. He is said to have migrated from the neighborhood of Delhi to *Bandipur* in *Faizabad,* where he made himself famous in his contests with the *Rajbhars.* This tradition obviously is not true because *Rajbhars* were defeated by early *Muslim* rulers. At best these people might have been settled by the early *Muslim* rulers in this area.

Generally speaking in Avadh, the origin of a clan of solar descent requires convincing proof of its genuineness. The lunar clans are often of true *Rajput* stock such as the *Janwars* of *Gonda* and *Bahraich* whose authenticity appears to be beyond question. The common story of *Rajput* taking service with a *Bhar* chief and then ousting his master is frequent in *Faizabad* as elsewhere. The common traditions are that a certain man was on a pilgrimage to Ayodhya or was accompanying a marriage procession to the place and that on the way he was molested by the *Bhars,* and afterwards returning with a force to punish the aggressors seized their lands for himself or again that a scion of some princely house, being driven eastwards by the Muslim invaders took service with the *Bhars,* and having risen to power by force of his superior breeding turned upon his master and slow him. These traditions are obviously fake because when early *Muslim* rulers came here, they were opposed by *Bhars*.

Such tales prevail throughout Avadh and are common in this district even with the *Bachhagotis*. They are obviously inventions of later years when a clan had become firmly established and required an account of the family history to serve as evidence of the illustrious descent of the reigning chieftain. It is going too far to assert that all these *Rajputs* are *Bhars* improved out of recognition but it may be suggested that these settlers, coming at a time when the *Hindu* caste system had not yet fully crystallized, mingled freely with the indigenous population. It is also possible that the conquest of the *Bhars* was not affected by a few isolated groups but rather by the armies of the Delhi *Sultans* in whose ranks there were many *Rajputs* and it is quite conceivable that the latter settled in the neighborhood of Ayodhya under the protection of its Muslim garrison. It is interesting to note that there are some traditions of this district which suggest that many Muslims colonized this place long before the *Rajputs*[14].

The first Muslim invaders of Avadh or Ayodhya is ascribed to the legendary hero *Saiyid Salar Masud Ghazi,* popularly known as *Ghazi Mian.* According to the *Mirat-i-Masudi* of *Abdur Rahman Chisti* (died 1683 A.D.), he is said to have occupied Avadh sometime before 1030 A.D. All among the old Lucknow road, there are numerous tombs which the local Muslims say are those of the followers of *Saiyid Salar*. There are near *Raunahi,* an ancient mosque and the graves of two martyrs, *Auliya* and *Makan Shabid.* It is said that an expedition came to Avadh in the reign of *Sultan Ibrahim* in 1080 A.D. If so, it might have been that of *Hajib Taghatigin* who crossed the *Ganga* and advanced into *Hindustan* further than any army since the time of *Mahmud* of *Ghazni.* In 1194 A.D, *Muiz-ud-din Muhammad Bin Sam* (commonly known as *Shihab-ud-din Ghori*) is said to have conquered Avadh after taking *Kannauj* and it is supposed that either he himself or one of his lieutenants occupied Ayodhya. It was in these times that *Shah Juran Ghori* lived here and his tomb is still pointed out at a site known as *Shah Juran ka Tila*.

It is not quite cleat when Ayodhya became the headquarters of a Muslim province in the kingdom of Delhi. *Minhaj Siraj,* a contemporary of the early *Turkish Sultans* of Delhi, has given an account of the different governors of Avadh who were appointed between 1206 and 1260 A.D. His work indicates that during the early Turkish rule Avadh remained a stronghold of powerful local Hindu *rajas* from whom the governors of the *Sultans* could obtain only nominal allegiance. These governors also used Avadh as a base for the extension of their territory further east and some of them gained immense power within a short period and challenged the authority of the *Sultans* who being very apprehensive of them, frequently transferred then from the *Subah.*

Qutub-ud-din Aibek assigned Avadh to *Malik Husam-ud-din Ughulbak* after 1193 A.D. The latter was joined by *Muhammad Bakhtiyar Khalji,* an enterprising general who having failed to attract the attention of *Sultan Muiz-ud-din Muhammad* and of *Qutub-ud-din Aibek,* shifted to *Badaun* and from there to *Avadh. Bakhtiyar Khalji* found a great outlet for his energies in *Avadh.*

Of all the governors of *Avadh* under the early *Turkish Sultans* in India, *Nasir-ud-din Mahmud* (the eldest son of *Sultan Shamsu-ud-din Iltutmish*), who was appointed in 1226 A.D., alone displayed feats of valour and organizing ability. He subdued a large number of local *Bhar* chieftains who had rallied all their strength to repel the growing menace of the *Turkish* invaders. He was succeeded by his brother *Malik Ghiyasuddin Muhammad* who rose in revolt in Avadh in 1236 A.D. against his elder brother; *Ruku-ud-din, Iltutmish's* successor. When *Razia* ascended the throne of Delhi (1236 A.D.), she assigned Avadh to *Malik Nusrat-ud-din Taisi* who took his forces to Delhi to help his sovereign against her rebellious nobles, but he fell ill and died before he could enter Delhi. *Qamar-ud-din Qiran* was appointed his successor. He made numerous raids into *Tirhut* and subdued the *rajas* of that locality. He was replaced by *Tughan Khan* in August, 1245 A.D. and in 1255 Avadh was assigned to *Qutlugh Khan* who had married *Mallika-i-Jahan,* the widow of *Iltutmish* and the mother of *Sultan Nasir-ud-din* but he was shortly afterwards ordered to move to *Bahraich. Qutlugh Khan* refused to obey and marched towards *Badaun. Malik Bektimur,* who was ordered by the *Sultan* to enforce obedience to the royal commands was defeated and killed by *Qutlugh Khan* at *Badaun.* The *Sultan* thereupon himself drove the rebel to *Bahraich.*

Qutlugh Khan's successor, *Malik Taj-ud-din Irsalan Khan,* also rebelled against the *Sultan* but had to sue for peace and was pardoned through the intercession of *Balban (Ulugh Khan).*

The *Tabqat-i-Nasiri* comes to an abrupt end after 1260 A.D. A great confusion prevailed in the later years of *Nasir-ud-din Mahmud's* reign and according to *Ziya-ud-din Barani* "the roads had become poor and infested with robbers in the doab and Avadh and all communications of the capital with the eastern provinces were secered." When *Balban* ascended the throne he brought the situation under control. The severe punishments inflicted on the governors and high officials made them submissive. *Habibat Khan* (one of the earliest governors of Avadh in the reign of *Balban*) was severely flogged and removed from office for having committed a murder under the influence of liquor.

Aitgin Mu-i-daraz Amin Khan, another governor of *Avadh,* was sent in 1279 A.D. to suppress *Tughril Beg* who had rebelled in *Lakhnauti,* but was defeated by the latter and for his failure. *Balban* had him hanged at the gate of Avadh. The *Sultan* himself marched against *Tughril.* He stayed in Avadh, ordering a general recruitment to the army and making arrangements for the commissariat. From here he led a huge army and a flotilla to *Lakhnauti.*

In 1287 A.D. *Balban* was succeeded by his grandson *Kaiqubad* whose father *Bughra Khan,* was then governor of *Lakhnauti.* The latter marched against his son with a large army and reached *Avadh. Kaiqubad* also advanced from Delhi to give battle to his father. The armies of the two encamped in Avadh on the opposite banks of *Ghaghra* but due to the intercession of influential nobles good sense prevailed and a reconciliation was effected.

Amir Ali Sar Jandar Hatim Khan held Avadh till the accession of *Jalal-ud-din Khalji,* against whom he rebelled along with *Malik Chhajju* in August-September 1290 A.D. The rebellion was crushed and *Malik Taj-ud-din Kuchi,* whose virtues have been extolled by *Barani,* was appointed *Amir Ali Sar Jandar's* successor but Avadh was shortly afterwards occupied by the *Sultan's* nephew *Ala-ud-din.* As he passed most of his time at *Kara. Avadh* began to suffer in importance. When *Ala-ud-din* was away on his *devgiri* expedition, *Avadh* and *Kara* was governed by *Ala-ul-Mulk.* On his return, *Ala-ud-din* ordered one of his lieutenants, *Zafar Khan* to proceed to Avadh and to make preparations there for escaping by boat to *Lakhnauti* if they were hard-pressed by his uncle, *Sultan Jalal-ud-din,* but *Ala-ud-din* succeeded in assassinating his uncle in *Kara* and sent his head to Avadh for public exhibition.

During the first year of his reign *Ala-ud-din* assigned Avadh and *Kara* to *Ala-ul-mulk* but the latter was soon recalled to Delhi. Later, the *Sultan* put Avadh and *Badaun* in the charge of his nephews, *Malik Umar* and *Manghu Khan,* but they rebelled against him. As the *Sultan* was then busy in reducing *Ranthambhor* to submission they were captured and sent to him there.

During the reign of *Muhammad Bin Tughlaq, Malik Ain-un-mulk Multani* was governor of *Avadh* and *Zafrabad* for a long time. He waged incessant war against the recalcitrant chieftains and on the whole peace and prosperity prevailed in Avadh during his regime. He was able to obtain the co-operation of the common people of the locality and when famine raged in Delhi and the greater part of the doab, provisions were sent for their relief from Avadh. The *Sultan* himself left Delhi and took up temporary residence in a village named *Swargdwari* in order to obtain provisions from Avadh easily. But *Ain-ul-mulk* became suspicious of the *Sultan's* designs and rebelled against him (1340 A.D.). According to *Ibn-i-Battuta* (who was an eye witness of these events) the *Sultan* was placed in a very difficult positions but the rebellion was quelled and *Ain-ul-mulk* was removed from Avadh. The name of his successor is not known but a Hindu, *Kishan Bazran Indri* was the governor of Avadh in the later part of the reign.

During his first expedition to Bengal in November 1353, *Sultan Firuz Tughlaq* halted in Avadh. The local Hindu chieftains and other nobles, who had become rebellions during the latter part of the reign of *Muhammad Bin Tughlaq* reached Avadh and offered their allegiance to the *Sultan*. During his second expedition to Bengal in 1358-59. *Firuz Shah* again stayed at Avadh and marched from there to *Zafrabad* where he founded *Jaunpur*. In 1376-77 *Malik Husam-ud-din Nawa* was appointed governor of *Avadh* and *Sandila* and after his death in 1377-78, his eldest son, *Malik Saif-ud-din* succeeded him as governor. He served *Firuz Shah* till the end of his reign and then joined *Sultan Muhammad Shah,* the younger son of *Firuz Shah* in April-May 1389. Great confusion prevailed in the Delhi Sultanate in the later part of *Firuz Shah's* reign and continued during the time of his successors, resulting in the decline of the central government in Delhi. In May 1394, *Sultan Mahmud Nasir-ud-din Shah* ordered *Malik-ush-sharq Khwaja-i-jahan* to proceed to *Hindustan* which then comprised the eastern regions of the Delhi *Sultanate*. He bought *Kannauj, Kara, Avadh, Sandila, Dalmau, Bahraich* etc. under subjugation and founded the independent *Sharqi* dynasty of *Jaunpur*.

Under the *Jaunpur* kings Avadh was administrated in a better way than under the later *Sultans* of Delhi. The local *zamindars* and *rajas* also appear to have strengthened their position and the *Sharqi* rulers has to placate them to maintain peace and order in their kingdom. It was in the reign of *Ibrahim Shah Sharqi* (1401-1440 A.D.) that *Mir Saiyid Muhammad Ashraf Jahangir Siffani* author of *Lataif-i-Ashrafi* and a number of important mystical works went from *Jaunpur* to *Kiehhauchha* and died there on 27th *Muharram* 808 H. (25th July 1405 A.D.). He is said to have exercised a great deal of influence on the local population.

From 1452 to 1480, *Bahlul* (the founder of *Lodi* dynasty of the *Afghans*) had to wage incessant war against the *Sharqi Sultans* before he could put an end to their power. Avadh again became a part of the *Sultanate* of Delhi and was given by *Bahlul* to an *Afghan* noble named *Kala Pahar Farmuli. Sultan Husain Sharqi,* an ambitious man took every opportunity to retrieve the ground he had lost. *Avadh* and *Jaunpur* remained in the disturbed condition till about 1495, when *Sikander Lodi* was able to consolidate his empire as far as Bihar. But peace was short-lived, for many *Afghan* nobles were alienated from his successor, *Ibrahim Lodi.* In the early years of the latter's reign a civil war broke war between the *Sultan* and his brother, *Jalal Khan* whose followers defeated *Said Khan,* son of *Mubarak Khan Lodi* of *Awadh.* But *Jalal Khan's* power could not last very long and Avadh again came under the sway of *Ibrahim Lodi.*

On the eve of *Babur's* invasion, *Bayazid Farmuli* held Avadh. After *Ibrahim Lodi's* death in the battle of *Panipat* (1526), he, with a number of other Afghan chiefs, joined *Babur* and a portion of Avadh, carrying a large amount of revenue was assigned to him by *Babur.* But he soon rebelled against his new master who himself hastened towards the east in February 1528 ordering *Chin Timur Sultan* to proceed in advance to crush the rebels. The latter reached Avadh as a result of which *Bayazid* and his family escaped to *Ghazipur. Babur* himself reached Avadh and stayed there for a few days and was greatly impressed with the "gardens, running water, well designed buildings, tress, particularly mango trees and various birds of colored plumage". He appointed *Baqi Tashqandi* the governor of Avadh, who subdued the rebellious local chiefs. During his regime *Baqi* built a mosque in Ayodhya in 1528. The inscription inside the mosque gives the date of the construction of the building in the last line and is as follows:

Ba farmuda-i-Shah Babur ki adlash
Bina ist ta kakh-i-gardun mulaqi
Bina kard in muhbit-i-qudsiyan
Amir-i-saadat-nishan Mir Baqi
Burad khair baqi-chu sal-i-binaish
Agan shud ke guftam-bucad khair baqi

Humayun succeeded *Babur* and his campaigns against *Gujurat* let loose a spate of troubles in the eastern regions of his empire. *Muhammad Zaman Mirza, Sultan Mirza* and *Ulugh Beg Mirza* rebelled in the eastern districts. *Ulugh Beg Mirza* and his sons captured Avadh and tried to occupy *Jaunpur* and *Kara Manikpur. Hindal,* the younger brother of *Humayun,* immediately left *Agra* and hastened towards the east to crush this rebellion but the *Mirzas* banded together and prepared to give battle in the vicinity of Ayodhya. *Ulugh Beg Mirza* and his sons fought desperately but were defeated.

Avadh again came under the authority of the Afghans after the overthrow of the *Mughals* by *Shershah* who established his mint here which remained in use even after the restoration of *Mughal* rule. Avadh and the eastern regious of the empire remained in a disturbed condition during the early years of Akbar's reign. In 1564-65 Avadh is mentioned as *jagir* of *Sikander Khan Khan-i-Alam,* while *Ibrahim Khan,* uncle of *Ali-Quli Khan-i-Zaman* held *Surhurpur.* They rebelled in concert with *Khan-i-Zaman* but the rebellion was suppressed by Akbar personally. In 1566, *Khan-i-zaman* was pardoned but he soon rebelled again. Ayodhya was held on his behalf by *Sikander Khan*, who was besieged there in the fort in 1567 by *Muhammad Quli Khan Barlas, Raja Todar Mal* and other important nobles of the imperial army. On account of the defeat and death of *Ali Quli Khan* and the pressure of the besiegers, *Sikander Khan* fled towards *Gorakhpur*. The *sirkar* of Awadh was assigned to *Muhammad Quli Khan Barlas* in 1567 and *Munim Khan Khan-i-Khanan,* the governor of the eastern districts returned to *Jaunpur*. *Muhammad Mohsin Khan,* who was then in charge of the old *pargana* of *Sinjhauli* is said to have founded the town of *Akbarpur* where he also built a fort and a mosque.

The eastern region of the empire appears to have remained tranquil for some time and no reference to Avadh is available in the contemporary chronicles. In 1580-81, *Wazir Khan* of *Herat* was appointed governor of Avadh. *Abul Fazal* says, "As that province was without a great officer, his majesty ordered that the peasantry and soldiers should be succored. He went off in the end of the month and many choice servants and soldiers accompanied him".

In 1580 *Tarsun Muhammad Khan* was appointed governor of *Jaunpur* in place of *Masum Khan Farankhudi* who had become rebellious and had to be transferred in Avadh in consequence although this did not cause him to abandon his evil designs. *Arab Bahadur, Niabat Khan* and other dissatisfied nobles joined him. *Shahbaz Khan,* governor of Bihar was sent to reduce him to submission and a fight occurred near *Sultanpur Bilheri* on January 22, 1581. *Shahbaz Khan* was forced to retired to *Jaunpur* but *Tarsun Muhammad Khan* surprised the rebels and compelled them to flee. He and *Shahbaz Khan* advanced against *Masum Khan* and again a battle took place in the neighborhood of Avadh. *Masum Khan* was defeated and fled toward the *Shivalika* hills. *Peshrau Khan* received the governor ship of Avadh in the place of *Masum Khan Farankhudi* but he too soon revolted and fell into disgrace. In 1582 and subsequent years the army of Avadh under *Khan-i-Azam Mirza Azizi Koka* was sent to suppress the rebellion in Bihar and Bengal.

In 1585 grain became cheap and peasantry found it difficult to pay the government revenue in money. "His Majesty remitted in the provinces of Allahabad, Oudh and Delhi, one in 5½ shares of the spring crop and one-fifth share in the *haveli* of Allahabad. For the autumn crop, he remitted one-sixth in the provinces of Oudh and Allahabad". Next year again a great fall in prices of grains was registered in Allahabad, Oudh and Delhi. Consequently, Akbar remitted one-sixth of the revenue. "A multitude of men", says Abul Faz, "obtained relief and formed assemblies for thanksgiving and rejoicings".

In 1586 the system of appointing two amirs as governors of a province was started so that at least one could always remain activity engaged in the administration of the place in the absence of the other. Consequently Avadh was assigned to *Fateh Khan* and *Qasim Ali; Mulla Nazir* and *Tora Chand* were attached with them as dawn and *Bakshi. Fateh Khan* died in 1589-90. In 1594-95 a new experiment in administration was made and a *vazir* was appointed in each province. *Kansur or Khanaur* was appointed *vazir* in Avadh. In Akbar's reign the empire was systematically divided into provinces and the administrative arrangements introduced by him remained undisturbed during the reign of *Jahangir* and his successors. References to Avadh became very scantly in the contemporary chronicles. William Finch, the English merchant, who travelled through the Mughal Empire (1608-11) says that "Avadh is a city of ancient note, and seat of a Poten King now much ruined, the castle built four hundred years ago. Here are also the ruins of *Ranichand's* castle and houses, which the Indians acknowledge for the great God saying that he took flesh upon him to see the *tamasha* of the world. In the ruins *Ramayan* certain *Brahmins,* who record the names of all such, Indians as wash themselves in the river running thereby; which custom they say, hath continued four lac of years. Some two miles on the further side of the river is a cave of his with a narrow entrance, but so spacious and full of turnings within that a man well loose himself there, if he take not better heed; where it is thought his ashes were buried. Hither resort many from all parts of India, which carry from hence in remembrance certain grains of rice as black as gunpowder, which they say have been reserved over since. Out of the ruins of this castle is yet much gold tryed. Here is great trade and such abundance of Indian ass-horne that they make hereof bucklers and divers sort of drinking cups. There are of these hornes, all the Indian allirme, some rare of great price, no jewell comparable, some esteeming them the right uncertain horne".

In the reign of *Jahangir, Baqir Khan Najm Sani* was appointed governor of Avadh in 1621 A.D. In 1621-22 he rendered valuable service to *Jahangir* and resisted the rebel prince *Khurram (Shah Jahan).*

Mirza Khan Manuchehr, a grandson of *Abdur Rahim Khan-i-Khana,* was appointed governor of Avadh in the tenth year of *Shah Jahan's* reign, but he lived there for only a short period. The name of his successor is not known but in the twenty-sixth year of his reign *Shah Jahan* appointed *Mirza Badi-uz-Zaman Shah Nawaz Khan,* governor of Avadh and also assigned to him *Gorakhpur* and *Bahraich.* He remained in Avadh for five years and was succeeded by *Shafi-ullah Tarbiat Khan Barlas* who was soon recalled to the capital owing to the war of succession which had commenced.

Iradat Khan Mir Ishaq was appointed *faujdar* of Avadh in 1658 but he died that very year and *Azim Khan Koka* was appointed as *faujdar* of Avadh and Gorakhpur in his place. He was succeeded by *Shah Quli Khan* who died in Ayodhya in the tenth year of *Aurangzeb's* reign. Thevenot, who travelled in India in 1666-67, was informed that there are many *rajas* who did not own the authority of the great Mughal and that there were two "Pagodas of great reputation in Avadh". In 1670, *Tarbiat Khan* was again appointed governor of Avadh in place of *Fidai Khan,* but he did not remain in office more than a year. *Saadat Khan* succeeded him in 1675 and was later replaced by *Namdar Khan. Khwaja Mir Khwafi Salabat Khan* was appointed *subehdar* in 1684 but shortly afterwards *Namdar Khan* was reappointed to succeed him.

In February 1690, *Himmat Khan* was appointed *subedar* of Avadh and *faujdar* of Gorakhpur. In 1694 new appointments and transfers were made again. *Askar Khan* succeeded *Himmat Khan* in October 1694. He remained there till January 1698, and was replaced by *Zabardast Khan. Khuda Banda Khan Bayutat* received the governorship of Avadh in October 1700. In December, 1703, *Shamsher Khan* was made governor of Avadh probably called *Moazzamabad Avadh* at that time. He was succeeded by *Mirza Khan-i-Alam* who died in July 1706 and *Abu Nasar Khan* obtained the governorship of Avadh in the same year. According to the author of *Khulasat-ut Tawarikh,* the province was famous for its excellent rice and extensive cultivation. "In the environs of Ayodhya, gold was obtained by shifting dust. Fish was speared by men in boats on the river *Sai* ".

In 1712, *Bahadur Shah* the emperor, appointed *Mir Qamar-ud-din subehdar* of Avadh and *Faujdar* of Lucknow and also conferred on him the title of *Khan-i-Dauran Khan Bahadur* in the same year but shortly afterwards he resigned.

In the reign of *Jahandar Shah,* the governor of Avadh was once again conferred upon *Mir Qamar-ud-din Khan-i-Dauran* who enjoyed this position only for a short time till the first year of *Farrukh Siyar's* reign (1713 A.D.) when *Mubariz-ul-Mulk Mir Muhammad Sarbuland Khan Dilawar Jang* was appointed governor. He is in turn was soon removed from office and recalled to court. In 1719, *Girdhar Nagar* nephew of *Chhabila Ram,* was made governor of Avadh with very extensive powers. He remained in office till the downfall of *Saiyid* brothers of *Barha.* The coins struck in the mint of Avadh during the reign of *Muhammad Shah* had the words Avadh and Akhtar Nagar inscribed on them. The end of *Girdhar Nagar's* governorship in Seprtember 1722, saw the decline of Avadh and it soon became a bone of contention among several local chieftains. It was his successor, *Saadat Khan Burhan-ul-mulk,* who in the reign of *Muhammad Shah,* was able to maintain peace and order in Avadh and thus extended his power considerably[15].

The founder of the ruling dynasty of Avadh, *Mir Muhammad Amin,* entitled *Saadat Khan Burhan-ul-Mulk,* who traced his descent from the seventh *Imam* of the *Shias,* was a native of *Nishapur* in *Khurasan.* In 1708-09, he migrated to India in search of employment. In July 1710, he entered the service of *Sarbuland Khan, faujdar* of *Kara-Manikpur* in Allahabad, but in 1712, he resigned due to some misunderstanding. From 1713, he remained in the service of Emperor *Farrukh Siyar.* On October 6, 1719, he was made the *faujdar* of *Hindaun Biana* by the next emperor *Muhammad Shah.* He had taken part in the intrigue connected with the over throw of *Saiyid* brothers who had sought to replace *Muhammad Shah* by *Muhammad Ibrahim.* In 1720, as a reward for his services, he was given the title of *Saadat Khan Bahadur* as also the governorship of Agra from which he was transferred to Avadh in 1722.

At that time the *subah* of Avadh was dominated by semi-independent and powerful *Zamindars* and *rajas* who possessed their own armies and strong brick or mud fortress. In the beginning of 1723, when one of these refused to surrender the *parganas* he had seized, *Saadat Khan* proceeded to crush his power and in the contest *Mohan Singh* died and his army fled from the field in the panic and *Saadat Khan* got back the *parganas*. The city of Lucknow which was in the occupation of the *Shaikhzadas,* was captured by him in 1722. In 1725, *Saadat Khan* started suppressing the other chiefs of Avadh and his success here as well as in other parts of the empire enhanced his prestige and established his reputation. He then carried out a fresh revenue settlement which increases the revenue of the province. For these services he was presented by the emperor with the *mansab* of 7,000 and honored with the title of *Burhan-ul-Mulk.* When *Nadir Shah* sacked Delhi in 1738-39, *Saadat Khan* was summoned to its defense by the emperor but soon after the capture of Delhi by *Nadir Shah, Saadat Khan* died on March 19, 1739.

Saadat Khan resided chiefly in Ayodhya where at *Lachhman Ghat,* a short distance from the town, he built the *Qila Mubarak* as his official residence. He had a strong army which was better equipped that of any noble in North India. Perhaps his greatest achievement was his victory over the *Marathas* at *Jalesar* in April 1737.

Till the time, the city of *Faizabad* had not been founded. There was a *keorah* jungle on the banks of river *Ghaghra* where the *Nawab* pitched his tent and held court, later converting this spot into a military cantonment. He also constructed a *bangla* around which he raises a mud wall with a bastion at each corner as in a fort. This enclosure was large enough to house his cavalry, infantry and artillery. The houses he built were of mud, probably because of the temporary nature of his tenure. After his death, in the time of *Safdar Jang,* this township came to be called *Faizabad,* and the headquarters of the government was transferred to this new city, the people continuing to call it *bangla.*

Saadat Khan was succeeded by his nephew and son-in-law. *Mirza Muhammad Muqim* who had already carried on the government of the *subah* when *Saadat Khan* had gone to Delhi. After *Saadat Khan's* death, he paid two crores of rupees to *Nadir Shah* and was confirmed as *subedar* of Avadh by *Muhammad Shah.* In addition, he was appointed *Mir-i-Atish* and was made *vazir* of the empire on the death of *Nizam-ul-mulk* and was dignified with honors and titles.

Safdar Jang was the real founder of the city of *Faizabad* and it was in his regime that it was completed. The sons of *Atma Ram* (a *diwam*) laid out a long *bazar* to the west of *Saadat Khan's* enclosure; *Ismail Khan,* a *risaldar,* built the market known as *Ismailganj;* and several other houses were built by traders and others and some Mughal chiefs laid out gardens as pleasure resorts. However, *Safdar Jang* himself stayed in Delhi for a considerable period.

Taking advantage of the change of government, the then *raja* of *Tiloi* made an attempt to regain the independence of which his ancestor had been deprived in 1723, but he was defeated by *Safdar Jang* in November 1739. Early in 1741, *Nawal Singh Gaur* of *Katesar* (district *Sitapur*) also revolted and *Safdar Jang* led a successful punitive expedition against him from *Faizabad.* The *raja* who fled without giving fight, later tendered his submission and accordingly his territory was restored to him.

Safdar Jang's most trusted *diwan* was *Raja Nawal Rai* who was killed on August 13, 1750 at *Khudaganj* in an engagement with the troops of *Ahmad Khan Bangash,* the *nawab* of *Farrukhabad.* Avadh remained in a disturbed condition for some time due to the incursions of the *Bangash* chiefs.

Shortly before his death *Safdar Jang* lost favor with the emperor and was dismissed from the office of *Vazir.* He died of cancer of the leg on October 5, 1754 and was buried in Delhi where a beautiful mausoleum was raised over his grave.

His son, *Shuja-ud-daula* succeeded him and made *Faizabad* his capital. When the emperor, *Alamgir II,* was murdered in 1759, his son *Shah Alam II,* fled for his life and took refuge with *Shuja-ud-daula.* When *Ahmad Shah Abdali* invaded Indian in 1761, at the invitation of *Najib-ud-daula, Shuja-ud-daula* won over to their side. But soon after the defeat of *Marathas,* in the battle of *Panipat,* he realized that he had made a mistake in joining the Afghans. After this battle, when the emperor was returning from Bihar having been routed by the British, he was received by *Shuja-ud-daula* in *Sarai Saiyid Razi* on July 19, 1761. He appointed *Shuja-ud-daula Vazir* of the empire on February 15, 1762, the latter thus regaining the honor his father had lost.

After sustaining a series of defeats at the hands of the British, *Mir Qasim* took refuge with *Shuja-ud-daula* who espoused his cause. *Shah Alam* was secretly corresponding with the British who were anxious to foment differences between the emperor and the *vazir* and wanted the latter to surrender *Mir Qasim* to them. The forces of *Mir Qasim, Shuja-ud-daula* and *Shah Alam II* were defeated by the British at *Baksar* on October 23, 1764. *Shah Alam II* at once cast his lot with the British and even issued a proclamation divesting *Shuja-ud-daula* of all authority and status. But the latter refused to come to terms until the British had marched on Lucknow and Allahabad and all Avadh was at their money.

On August 16, 1765, *Shuja-ud-daula* was eventually compelled to enter into a treaty, "for perpetual and universal peace, sincere friendship and firm union" with the East India Company. Clive restored the districts of Avadh to *Shuja-ud-daula* on consideration that "every motive of sound policy be weighed against extending the territorial possessions of the company". He thus strengthened Avadh as buffer state between Bengal and Northern India. *Kara* and Allahabad were taken away from Avadh and given to *Shah Alam II* for his own maintenance. *Shuja-ud-daula* had also to pay the fifty lac of rupees as a war indemnity to the Company and thus the kingdom of Avadh was gradually drawn into the meshes of the company.

In 1765, *Shuja-ud-daula* finally made *Faizabad* as his residence. He built a new, on a grander scale, the walls of *Saadat Khan's* old citadel. A deep trench was built around a vast plain extending for more than two miles on each side of the fort, which was reserved for his retainers and military officers. Later, in addition, two other large walls were built for the defense of the city. Most of the troops were posted night and day on the top of the walls. The city wall which was completed before 1722 was made of mud and was 30 feet thick, the top of the breastwork being 15 feet thick. *Shuja-ud-daula's* new mud fort and palace were still being built in January 1733 and are said to have employed 40,000 men daily in their construction. The walls of this new fort were sixty feet thick and "so well beat that Elephants made no impression with their feet". A grand market, *Chowk Bazar* extended from the southern gate of the fort to Allahabad gate of the city and was so broad that nearly ten bullock carts could ran abreast. It was entered through a handsome three-arched gateway. A visitor to the palace passed through *Chowk Bazar* and Macpherson, who visited *Faizabad* in 1773, was struck by the breadths of the streets but he noted that the houses on either side were of different construction. There were three well laid out flower and fruit gardens within the city walls; *Anguri Bagh* inside the fort. *Moti Bagh* situated in the heart of *Chowk Bazar* and *Lal Bagh,* the largest and the most beautiful, just outside the fort. There were two more gardens inside the walls, *Aish Bagh* and *Buland Bagh,* both on the western outskirts of the city.

Shuja-ud-daula paid special attention to the strengthening of his armed forces. He had about 80,000 foot regulars and 40,000 irregulars, the chief commander being *Saiyid Ahmad,* also known as *Bansiwala.* The chief officers of his cavalry were *Nawab Murtaza Khan Barij* and the two *Gosains, Himmat Bahadur* and *Umrao Gir.* After the battle of *Baksar, Shuja-ud-daula* reorganized his army dismissing most of the Mughal troops and enlisting *Rajputs,* other Hindus and Musalmans in their place. Gentil (the Frenchman), Aratoon (the Abyssinian) and some other officers of the note, who had served under the English and French, were commissioned to frame rules and regulations for the training and organizations of the artillery. An Arsenal was extablished in *Faizabad* under the supervision of good caliber and the latest design and lead shots and ammunition were manufactured here on a large scale. So efficient was this artillery that it was regarded as a serious menace to the company's security in Bengal. The *Nawab's* cavalry also had always been superior to that of the company.

He also had 22,000 messengers and a host of spies and his intelligence department was so efficient that he could obtain from all quarters the best and earliest information of every material event. *Ghulam Ali,* author of *Imad-us-Saadat,* estimates the total number of *harkaras* at 18000. So effectively did the department work that news from Poona reached *Faizabad* on the ninth day and from *Kabul* on the twelfth. He spent Rs 2, 16,000 annually on this important service.

During the regime of *Shuja-ud-daula, Faizabad* attained a prosperity which it never saw again. The merchants of Persia, Turan, China and Europe frequently visited the city with costly wares which they disposed of with profit. But the *Nawab* prohibited the export of gold and silver and all through maintained a favorable balance of trade. Grain, clothing and other articles of common necessity were more abundant and much cheaper in Avadh than in the territory under the English Company.

The East India Company continued its policy of transforming Avadh into a buffer state possessing only powers of intermediate resistance so that the *Marathas* and other invaders could be held at bay by the *Nawab* while the Company's troops were being rushed to his assistance. The British never intended that *Shuja-ud-daula* should become as powerful as to make his state a menace for them instead of a bulwark of defense. They became so alarmed that they decided to set some bounds to his military power, which would still enable him to maintain order within his territory and yet leave Avadh strong enough to serve them as a buffer against aggression. This led to a fresh treaty on November 29, 1768, when *Shuja-ud-daula* agreed but with great reluctance to limit his troops to 35,000 men.

At the time of Hasting's assumption of the governorship of Bengal, the East India Company was facing a severe deficit. As the districts of *Kara* and Allahabad were proving to be ruinously expensive, Hastings made them a source of profit by handing them back to *Shuja-ud-daula* on payment of sixty lakhs of rupees. To consolidate this deal a new treaty was concluded at Varanasi on September 7, 1773, by which *Shuja-ud-daula* agreed to have the Company's resident stationed at this court. Although this acquisition added to the revenues of Avadh, it also increased *Shuja-ud-daula's* reliance upon the English which in its turn intensified the friction between *Shuja-ud-daula* and the *Marathas*.

In 1774, being unable to recover from the *Rohillas* a sum of Rs. 40 Lakhs, *Shuja-ud-dauls* paid to the British this very amount and with the help of their troops destroyed the *Rohillas* and annexed their territory to Avadh.

Shuja-ud-daula fell ill and died in *Faizabad* on January 26, 1775. He was the first of his line whose body was interred there in the *Gulab Bari,* a mausoleum which is still an ornament to the place.

With his son *Asaf-ud-daula's* accession as *Nawab Vizir* (January 31, 1775), a great change took place in the politics of Avadh. According to *Kamal-ud-din Haider,* he transferred his capital to Lucknow seven years after his accession. *Faiz Bakhsh* in his *Tarikh-i-Farah Bakhsh* is however not clear on this point but it appears from his account that the process of transfer commenced from the very first year of the *Asaf-ud-daula's* accession. William Hocy in his translation of his work says, "All the equipment's and surroundings of wealth and grandeur were by degrees transferred to Lucknow and the cantonments and workshops and elephants, bullocks and everything connected with government and the state, gathered there. The market for the camp followers, troops and all servants of the government, old and new, left *Faizabad* and went to Lucknow.

In his reign, the East India Company, began to interfere actively in the affairs of Avadh. The *Nawab Vizir* was informed that the treaties between his father and the Company were no longer binding and he had to enter into the treaty of *Fyzabad* (May 21, 1775) which took the form of a defensive alliance, the main result of which was the deprivation of a considerable portion of his revenues.

As he could not meet the demand of the East India Company, he turned his eyes towards the treasure, estimated at more than twenty crores of rupees, which *Shuja-ud-daula* had left to his mother *Nawab Begum* and his wife *Bahu Begum*. *Bahu Begum,* eventually consented to give him thirty lakhs of rupees and to grant him a loan of twenty-six lakhs, on condition that he did not make any further demands on her and that she could not continue in the full enjoyment of her *jagirs* and property. *Bahu Begum* later accused the *Nawab* of refusing to comply with the terms of the agreement which had been guaranteed by John Bristow on the behalf of his company.

During the next six years or so, the internal affairs of the Avadh went from bad to worse. *Mukhtar-ud-daula,* the *vizir* was murdered and replaced by *Haider Beg Khan,* a man of Hasting's choice. In 1777, military expensed also increased substantially by the addition of a temporary brigade, a move which was not warranted but was motivated further to undermine the Nawab's prestige and power.

In 1778, *Asaf-ud-daula* requested the Company to remove this brigade and also complained of the continued exactions of the Company and the oppression and tyranny of its military officers. The request was granted on September 19, 1781, but only after a personal conference between Hastings and *Asaf-ud-daula* at *Chunar.* It was also decided that the agreement with the *Begums* was no longer valid and that the *Nawab* was to be allowed to resume all their *jagirs* and to seize the large treasure left by his father. Hastings, who badly in need of the money at this time, consented to this arrangement provided *Asaf-ud-daula* paid liberal pensions to the *Begums* and also gave rupees seventy lakhs to the Company.

It is said that in the nine years following 1774, the company had squeezed two crores and thirty lakhs of rupees out of the *Nawab.*

Asaf-ud-daula could not keep his promise of paying 70 lakhs to the Company. Hastings, therefore, instructed Middleton not to allow any negotiations or forbearance until the *Begums* went at the entire mercy of the *Nawab,* their *jagirs* in the quiet possession of the *amils,* and their wealth in such charge as might secure it against private embezzlement. Finally, Hastings made it quite clear that he wished all the *Nawab's* debts to the company to be discharged.

When the *Nawab* appointed his own *amils* to take charge of *Bahu Begum's jagirs,* she immediately defended them and strongly expressed her resentment in her letters to the resident. She said, "Should the country be lost to me it shall be lost to all. I give this intimation. Note it". In spite of this the resident sent a regiment to support the *amils* in the execution of the *Nawab's* commands and the *Nawab* announced his intention of proceeding to *Faizabad* to demand his father's treasure.

In the first week of January, 1782, British detachments were marched to Faizabad to support the *Nawab*'s troops. The fort was captured and the two eunuchs, who were the stewards of the Begums, were forced to part with the treasure and by January 28, 1782, the *Nawab* had taken possession of most of the treasure and had begun to pay off his debts to the Company.

The spoliation of the Begums of Avadh formed one of the charges in Hastings's impeachment on his return to England. According to the prosecution his conduct was criminal. Alfred Lyall says, "The employment, of personal severities, under the superintendence of British officer, in order to extract money from women and eunuchs, is an ignoble kind of undertaking, to cancel the guarantee and leave the *Nawab* to deal with the recalcitrant princesses was .justifiable, to push him on and actively assist, in measures of coercion against women and eunuchs was conduct unworthy and indefensible."

Hastings later tried to make some unsuccessful attempts to reorganize the administration and finances of the Avadh. Middleton was removed from the post of Resident and Bristow appointed in his place who ordered the withdrawal of the Company's regiment from Faizabad.

After the death of *Asaf-ud-daula. Bahu Begum* contemplated claiming a part in the management of Avadh and was encouraged by *Husain Raza Khan, Raja Tikait Rai, Almas Ali* and others. The *Begum's* request that the private treasure of *Asaf-ud-daula* he examined in the presence of some of her own people was not acceded to by the British Government, as they were apprehensive that she might lay claim to a part if not to the whole of it.

In 1808, *Bahu Begum* executed a will, making the British Government heir of the residue of her property, after reserving for her own purposes certain *jagirs*, pensions, etc., but the government declared its intention of yielding the inheritance to the *Nawab Vizir* of Avadh (*Saadat Ali Khan*). In 1813, *Bahu Begum* revoked her will and executed a deed of deposit making the then *Nawab Vizir, Ghazi-ud-din Haider*, her heir.

On her death in December, 18l5, property valued at about a crore of rupees was made over to the *Nawab* on his paying into the British treasury about 57 lakhs of rupees, the interest on the latter being earmarked (under the terms of the deed) for the payment of certain pensions. These pensions are now known as the *amanat wasikas* (trust pensions). There were certain other *jagirs* and pensions known as the *zamanat wasikas* (security pensions) payable from the Avadh treasury. But, in the case of diminution or resumption of the Avadh exchequer, the amount was to be made good from the residue of the *Begum's* property with the consent of the British Government.

Bahu Begum was 86 when she died. She passed the whole of her long life in splendor and state and was a woman of great distinction and rank, bearing and dignity. As Hocy has observed in his Memoirs, "No one woman in all the thirty-two *subahs* of India can he held up in these days as her rival in either the grandeur of her surroundings or the respect she could command. When at the zenith of her glory, she had ten thousand troops, formed by the *Kotwal* that a fakir with his followers was in the sarai of the town, that crowds were visiting him and that there was on evident intention on the part of the fakir to start a riot and cause dissension among the people. Thurburn immediately set out for the scene of disturbance accompanied by the *Kotwal* and 4 or 5 *burkundazes* (matchlock men) and ordered the *maulvi* and his followers to surrender their arms assuring him that the arms would be returned if he departed from the city. The fakir retorted that he could not and would not give up his arms as he had received them from his *pir* (spiritual guide). Neither could Forbes, the deputy commissioner, who visited him on February 17, persuade him to surrender Military aid was summoned but though the *maulvi* and his followers fought desperately they were arrested and placed under military guard. The Indian sepoys, however, had full sympathy with him and he was provided with all comforts in the jail.

At the end of May, 1857, the garrison of Faizabad consisted of a large force of Indian troops comprising the 22nd Bengal Infantry under Colonel Lennox, the 6th Oudh Irregular Infantry, commanded by Lieutenant Colonel O'Brien, a squadron of the 15th Irregular Cavalry, a battery of horse artillery under Major Mills and a company of the 7th Bengal Artillery. The European officers wore under no delusions as to the probability of the outbreak, and preparations were made in May to organize a scheme of defense by collecting stores and fortifying the house of Thurburn, the assistant commissioner. The British expected that the *zamindars* and pensioners would lend their assistance to them and this belief was encouraged by the offer of an asylum by *Raja Mau Singh, Thakur Raghunath Kunwar, Mir Dawar Husain* and *Nadir Shah*. A similar offer was made by the *mahants* of *Hanuman-garhi*, who from the first exerted themselves to keep their troops ready. But the British soon found that the assistance of the *zamindars* was not to be relied upon as they were unfit to resist the disciplined and well equipped Avadh forces. In these circumstances the British tried to send their families to Lucknow but when this proved impossible, owing to the uprisings in the *Daryabad* district, they were sent to *Shahganj* at the beginning of June where *Raja* Man *Singh* gave them shelter.

Meanwhile the sepoys had already reached *Faizabad* from *Azamgarh, Jaunpur* and *Varanasi*. They are said to have received a message from the king of Delhi to the effect that he had possession of the whole country and summoning them to rally round his standard. The sepoys contended that they were strong enough to turn the British out of the country and intended to do so and the 15th Irregular Cavalry left no means untried to induce the other regiments to kill their officers. The open struggle against the British commenced from the night of June 8. However some sepoys of the Artillery (the 22nd Native Infantry and the 6th Irregular Infantry), refused to injure the Europeans and even gave them money and assisted them in procuring a few boats to proceed down the *Ghaghra*.

They first plundered the treasury of nearly two and a quarter lakhs of rupees and then followed the usual practice, of releasing the prisoners from jail, one of whom was *Maulvi Ahmad Ullah Shah* who came to be known as the *Maulvi* of *Faizabad*. The main leaders were the *risaldar* of the 5th Troops 15th Irregular Cavalry and *Daleep Singh, subedar* of the 22nd Infantry, a *Chauhan Rajput* of *Baragaon* in the *Faizabad* district. They selected the *maulvi* as their leader and marched towards Lucknow, the government, of *Faizabad* being entrusted to *Raja Man Singh*. A battle was fought at *Chinhat* where the British forces were completely routed.

The sepoys held sway in the town of Faizabad and the local chieftains and *talukdars* found themselves in a state of practical independence, particularly Man Singh, who forthwith recovered his lost possessions and resumed his former position of importance. His attitude was doubtful and lie tried to be friendly with both sides.

Other *talukdars*, almost without exception, espoused the cause of the sepoys. This was notably the ease with the *Palwars* of *Birhar*, the *Bachhgotis* of *Hasanpur*, *Ram Sarup* of *Khapra Dih, Taffazzul Husain* of *Sammanpur* and the *Bhale Sultans*. The only exception was *Raja Rustam Shah*, the *Rajkumar* chieftain of Dora. The others, notably the *Chauhans*, whose stronghold was the fort of *Ghatampur* near *Baragaon*, joined actively against the British. At *Naurahi* the European fugitives from *Faizabad* were robbed by *Udit Narain Singh*, the eldest son of *Mahip Narain* of *Chandipur*. Further down the river at Chahora they were again stopped by *Madho Prashad Singh* of *Haswar* who afterwards took up arms against the British. The *talukdars* of Faizabad, like those of other places, extended their full support to the Avadh *darbar*, from its very establishment to the final restoration of British authority in Avadh and some of them even took the field in person.

Man Singh reached Lucknow in August, 1857, and the terms offered by him to the Avadh *darbar* were accepted. His match- lockmen were most active in the attack on the Residency where he tenaciously resisted the onslaught of General Neill who was killed in the encounter, Man Singh himself being wounded in two places.

Mahdi Husain was appointed *nazim* of Sultanpur by the Avadh darbar and he appointed *tehsildars* and *sazawals* in the territories under him. *Saiyid Ghulam Husain* (son of *Muhammad Husain*) was appointed *chakledar* of *Aldemau. Ismail Khan*, who was formerly a *tahsildar* (on behalf of the Company) at *Dostpur*, was appointed as his deputy. From *Shahzadpur* the latter planned attacks on the neighboring eastern district which was supported by many *talukdars* including the. *Rajkumars Amresh Singh* and *Chandresh Singh* (under the leadership of *Madho Prasad* and *Kishan Prasad*) who espoused the cause of the Avadh *durbar*. A large number of villagers were also most zealous in their support. In the first week of October, 1857, an attack on *Jaunpur* was planned by *Mahdi Husain* who raised 12,000 new troops which were joined by many villagers. Meanwhile orders were received from the Avadh *durbar* that as soon as *Jai Lal Singh* son of *Ghalib Jang*, *nazim* of *Azamgarh* and *Jaunpur*, reached Faizabad, the Sultanpur and Gorakhpur *nazims* were also to join him in an attack on *Azamgarh* and *Jaunpur*. *Mansab Ali* of *Sarai Mir* (district *Azamgarh*) who was appointed commandant of the regiment, reached *Kataria* with *Beni Madho* of *Atrauli* and a large force. A workshop was also established at Faizabad for the repair of heavy guns. A number of important centers were thus established throughout Faizabad by the forces of the Avadh durbar.

Faizabad remained completely independent till the end of January, 1858. But *Maharaja Jang Bahadur* of Nepal, an ally of the British, having occupied Gorakhpur on January 6, 1858, with his forces marched towards Faizabad on February 14 and reached *Berari* on the *Ghaghra* in the *Basti* district five days later. General Rowcroft, who had come up the river from Bihar with the Pearl naval brigade, some Nepalese troops and four guns, arrived within four miles of *Berari* on the 19th and the next day he was joined by a Nepalese brigade. He was then ordered lo bring up his boats to *Phulpur* (near *Tanda*), and hearing that this place was occupied by the forces of the *Avadh* durbar he attacked them and captured three of their guns. Thus *Jang Bahadur* was enabled to cross into Avadh leaving Rowcroft in command at *Gorakhpur*. Two days prior to Rowcroft's arrival at *Berari*, Captain Sotheby, who was escorting the boats up the river, had captured the well-protected *Palwar* stronghold of *Chandipur* in the extreme cast of the district, this being the first military action that took place in Faizabad since the outbreak of the struggle. *Maharaja Jang Bahadur* marched from *Phulpur* towards *Sultanpur* through the district, storming the small hut strong fort of *Bihrozpur* (near *Akbarpur*) which was bravely held by 34 men of *Umresh Singh* who were all killed. Thus the British secured the road as far as the *Gomati* and Rowcroft, who remained to the north of the *Ghaghra*, advanced as far west as *Amorha* (in *Basti*), only eight miles from Ayodhya.

Man Singh actually retired to *Shahganj* in February, 1858. He continued to negotiate with the Avadh durbar, but he was required by them to support their cause personally. He could, therefore, no longer afford to play a dual role and on March 10, 1858, he tendered his submission to the British and was allowed to return home on agreeing that he would report to them at Lucknow within 10 days. However, before he could proceed he was besieged by the Avadh forces in his fort at *Shahganj*. Strong and vigilant pickets were established by the Avadh forces on the river *Ghaghra*, opposite Ayodhya. Though Rowcroft remained at *Amorha*, the Avadh forces began to muster their strength in their camp at *Behra*. The eastern part of the Faizabad district was entirely under the influence of the *Palwars* and of *Kunvar Singh* of *Bihar* (who was then approaching *Azamgarh*), On March 29, 1858, Lugard left Lucknow for *Azamgarh* by way of Sultanpur and *Kunwar Singh* had to retire southwards in the direction of

Ghazipur. This, however, did not weaken the position of the Avadh forces in Faizabad and Rowcroft was thrown back from *Amorha* and had to withdraw to Captainganj.

After the battle of *Nawab*gunj in June, 1858, Hope Grant proceeded to the relief of Man Singh who was still besieged in his fort by a strong Avadh force of about 20,000 people. By the end of July the Avadh forces abandoned the siege and left *Shahganj*. They divided themselves into three parties, one joined *Begum Hazrat Mahal* in *Gonda*, and another went to *Sultanpur* and the third to *Tanda. Tanda, Jalalpur* and *Akbarpur* continued to remain the strong centre of the *Avadh* forces.

On October 11, Hope Grant marched from Lucknow and proceeded towards *Tanda* and three days later he reached *Akbarpur*. On the same day Colonel Simson and Major Raikes reached *Jalalpur*. Colonel Payne reached Silka and *Man Singh, Bhadesa*. The British forces held the line from Sultanpur (through *Pratapgarh*) to Allahabad and also from Sultanpur north to Faizabad to prevent the Avadh forces from entering the Sultanpur-Faizabad line into the Azamgarh district. Campbell began his operations by strengthening the Sultanpur position and detached Hope Grant, so that he could co-operate with a column advancing under Kelly from Azamgarh into Faizabad. Kelly was able to secure Akbarpur and then Tanda, where he halted on October 30, to guard Campbell's eastward flank during the ensuing operations. Raikes came upon some 4,000 Avadh forces in the act of crossing the Tons, but they retired into a jungle and their chief (*Fazl-i-Ali*) was also able to escape without being captured. Hope Grant returned to Sultanpur on October 23. Kelly was left in charge of Faizabad and was made responsible for the territory between Tanda and Sultanpur. On the other flanks also the British were making headway.

After *Beni Madho's* escape from his fortress of *Shankarpur*. His troops were driven northwards across the *Ghaghra* through the west of these districts. Hope Grant followed in pursuit and reached Faizabad where 4,300 men were collected under Colonel Taylor. The Avadh forces were entrenched beyond the *Ghaghra*. The British effected the crossing on November 27 by a bridge constructed under long-range fire by Captain Nicholson and drove their opponents into *Gonda*.

On December 5, Campbell started from Lucknow with a very strong- infantry division, a cavalry brigade and some 14 guns en route to Faizabad by way of *Nawab*ganj (*Barabanki*). Gradually by the end of the month the entire district submitted to the superior military resources of the British army[16].

Like other districts of the State the history of Faizabad after the reoccupation is mainly a history of administrative changes and national awakening.

The year 1916 is memorable for the inauguration of the Home Rule League founded by *Lokamanya Tilak* and branches were also established at Faizabad and Ayodhya.

In 1919 the British Government passed the Rowlatt Act which did away with the ordinary legal procedure for authorizing imprisonment only after trial. In protest *Gandhiji* organized a passive resistance movement and during his countrywide tour, came to Faizabad, Ayodhya and Tanda in 1920. A wave of unrest spread over many parts of the district and there were violent out-breaks in the *Birhar pargana* of the *Tanda* tehsil against the *zamindars* and the sympathizers of the British regime. A district Congress Committee was also formed in Faizabad in 1920.

The influence of the *Khilafat* Movement was also felt in the district in 1921. A meeting was held in *Khaspur mohalla* in Faizabad town which was attended by the Ali brothers and their mother. An office of the *Khilafat* Movement was established in the *Chowk* which was served by Hindus and Muslims alike.

Faizabad also took an active part in the Non-cooperation Movement and in the boycott of the courts, of foreign goods and the picketing of liquor shops.

In 1921-22, what was known as the *Kisan* Movement spread in the Faizabad district especially in the Tanda and Akbarpur tehsils because of the ill-treatment of their tenants by the zamindars. The *Kisans* of Faizabad co-operated with those of the Rae Bareli and Pratapgarh districts.

Jawaharlal Nehru also came to Faizabad in connection with this movement and addressed a large gathering of *kisans* at several places. In February, 1930, the Civil Disobedience Movement had gained so much ground in this district that the district officer of Faizabad was told to be very careful in case Jawaharlal Nehru or any other Congress leader visited these areas and that the movement should be suppressed as vigorously as possible.

Gandhi's famous salt march to *Dandi* in 1930 was the signal for action *on a* large scale. In Faizabad salt was prepared in defiance of the law near the Clock tower ill the *Chowk* and many persons were arrested for breaking the salt laws.

When Motilal Nehru died on February 7, 1931, a complete *hartal* was observed at Faizabad and *satyagrah* was offered when the government tried to ban this *hartal*.

On January 1, 1931, the working committee of the Congress adopted a resolution for the renewal of the Civil Disobedience Movement and the boycott of British goods. Jawaharlal Nehru started a countrywide campaign for this purpose and revisited Faizabad. On his arrival another *Kisan* conference was held in the town.

The Civil Disobedience Movement dragged on till May, 1934 and in 1935 the Congress decided to work the reforms introduced by the India Act of 1935 by contesting the elections to be held under the Act, both for the State and Central Legislatures. In Faizabad the Congress won two seats out of three, the third seat going to the Muslim League. The Congress also celebrated its golden jubilee all over the country and a public meeting was held on December 28, 1935, in *Akbarpur*.

In 1938, a provincial conference was held in Ayodhya under the president ship of Jawaharlal Nehru, *Acharya* Narendra Dev being the chairman of the reception committee. Thousands of *kisans* (peasants) attended this conference and a *khadi* exhibition was also organized on this occasion.

On the outbreak of the war in 1939, the Congress raised its voice against the recruitment of Indians for war service and meetings were held in Faizabad to publicize this stand.

The *Gandhi Ashram* at *Raniwan* (in Akbarpur), which was the centre of the *Khadi* industry, was now suspected of anti-British activities and was searched many times. The workers of the Ashram assisted the *Satyagrah* movement. In October, 1940, a huge meeting was organized at *Gosainganj* which was addressed by Jawaharlal Nehru who was then touring the eastern districts of the State with the avowed intention of stirring up agrarian discontent and strengthening the cause of *satyagrah*. Kamala Nehru Bhawan at Faizabad, a centre of the nationalist movement, stalwartly fostered and furthered satyagrah activities.

The Quit India Movement launched on August 8, 1942, followed by the arrest of *Gandhiji* and other prominent Congressmen, brought about a complete lack of leadership resulting in violent uprisings. On August 10, the students of the local institutions in Faizabad marched round the city. The deputy commissioner had the schools closed and there was a general upheaval. On August 23, 1942, the village of Raja Sultanpur in *Jahangiraganj* Thana, areas in its vicinity and parts of the *Azamgarh* district made spirited demonstrations which were ruthlessly suppressed by the government. On August- 28. 1942, trouble started on the southern side of *Tanda* between the *Baskhari* and *Jalalpur* police stations. In the villages of *Para* and *Gaura Mohammadpur*, incidents of cutting of telegraph wires between *Zafarganj* and the *Malipur* railway station were reported and many persons were arrested

With the end of the war in 1945, political prisoners were released and in 1946 the general elections were held, the Congress emerging ns the leading party and winning in Faizabad district two seats, the third once again going to the Muslim League. On July 1, 1947, the Indian Independence Bill was passed. The wheel had come full circle and India gained her independence on August 15, 1947[17].

Gazetteer of Archaeological Sites

Following is the gazetteer of sites falling under Police Stations Khandasa, Mawai, Patranga and Rudauli district Ayodhya.

P.S. Khandasa District Ayodhya

Ajrauli: The village lies on latitude 81⁰52′ N and longitude 26⁰35′40″ E. It lies 12 km from the P.S. The area of the mound is 2 acre. Height of the mound is 1 meter. The ceramic industries found are NBP, EM and LM.

Amawa Sufi: The village lies on latitude 81⁰50′ N and longitude 26⁰41′45″ E. It lies 12 km from the P.S. The mound lies at a distance of west of village. The area of the mound is 0.4 acre. Height of the mound is 0.6 meter. The ceramic industries found are OCP, G, EM and LM.

Bahitara: The village lies on latitude 81⁰53′10″ N and longitude 26⁰40′20″ E. It lies 12 km to the east of the P.S. The mound lies at a distance of 0.3 km to the west of village. The area of the mound is 5 acre. Height of the mound is 1.6 meter. *Pokhara* is located near the mound. The ceramic industry found is LM.

Bakauli: The village lies on latitude 81⁰48′40″ N and longitude 26⁰40′30″ E. It lies 15 km to the north of the P.S. The mound lies at a distance of 0.1 km to the south of village. The area of the mound is 1.4 acre. Height of the mound is plain. *Pahalwan Baba ka Sthan* is located on the mound and *Nesi Tara Talaab* is lies near the mound. The ceramic industry found is LM. This mound is ascribed to *Bhars*[18].

Bakchuna: The village lies on latitude 81⁰45′20″ N and longitude 26⁰37′ E. It lies 6 km from the P.S. The mound lies at a distance of 0.8 km to the west of village. The area of the mound is 6 acre. The ceramic industries found are OCP and LM.

Bhakhauli: The village lies on latitude 81⁰48′45″ N and longitude 26⁰40′35″ E. It lies 14 km to the north of the P.S. The mound lies to the north of the village. The area of the mound is 6.4 acre. Height of the mound is 7 meter. *Sagra Talaab* lies near the mound. The ceramic industries found are OCP, NBP and K.

Bhawan Nagar: The village lies on latitude 81⁰51′ N and longitude 26⁰40′30″ E. It lies 16 km to the north of the P.S. The mound lies at a distance of 0.1 km to the north of village. The area of the mound is 3 acre. Height of the mound is 3.3 meter. *Phalahari Baba ka Sthan* is located on the mound. The ceramic industry found is LM. There are remains of small mud floor on the mound[19].

Binayakpur: The village lies on latitude 81⁰47′10″ N and longitude 26⁰39′50″ E. It lies 1 km to the east of the P.S. The mound lies at a distance of 01 km to the west of village. The area of the mound is 6 acre. *Badri Singh Baghiya* is located on the mound. The ceramic industry found is LM.

Chirauli: The village lies on latitude $81^{0}52'40''$ N and longitude $26^{0}38'20''$ E. It lies 12 km to the north-east of the P.S. The mound lies to the north of the village. The area of the mound is 3 acre. Height of the mound is 1.6 meter. *Shiva Mandir* is located on the mound. The ceramic industry found is LM.

Dharauli: The village lies on latitude $81^{0}48'30''$ N and longitude $26^{0}37'40''$ E. It lies 3 km to the north-west of the P.S. The mound lies at a distance of 0.8 km to the east of village. The area of the mound is 05 acre. The ceramic industry found is OCP.

Dhilli Saraiya: The village lies on latitude $81^{0}52'$ N and longitude $26^{0}41'30''$ E. It lies 12 km to the north of the P.S. The mound lies to the north of village. The area of the mound is 3 acre. The ceramic industry found is OCP.

Dholi Askaran: The village lies on latitude $81^{0}52'$ N and longitude $26^{0}39'$ E. It lies 15 km to the north of the P.S. The area of the mound is 3 acre. Height of the mound is 1.6 meter. *Sagra Talaab* lies near the mound. The ceramic industry found is Late Chalcolithic of corded ware tradition.

Gahnag (Majra Rai Patti): The village lies on latitude $81^{0}49'30''$ N and longitude $26^{0}39'30''$ E. It lies 07 km to the north-west of the P.S. The mound lies at a distance of 0.1 km to the west of village. The area of the mound is 16 acre. Height of the mound is 2 meter. The bricks of sizes 9x8x2, 10x9x2.5 and 8x7x2.5 inch are found on the mound. *Shri Gahnar Dev Baba ks Sthan* lies on the mound and *Bandhawa* Lake is located near the mound. The ceramic industry found is LM.

Ghatauli: The village lies on latitude $81^{0}50'30''$ N and longitude $26^{0}36'40''$ E. It lies 9 km to the north of the P.S. The mound lies at a distance of 0.5 km to the west of village. The area of the mound is 3 acre. Height of the mound is 1.3 meter. The bricks of sizes 7x5x2.5 inch are found on the mound. *Shiva Mandir* and *Navdiha* Lake are found on and near the mound respectively. The ceramic industries found are NBP and LM.

Kariya ka Purwa (Mahra Rautawa): The village lies on latitude $81^{0}48'36''$ N and longitude $26^{0}36'20''$ E. It lies 8 km to the east of the P.S. The mound lies to the east of the village. The area of the mound is 0.4 acre. *Bhagwaan Taal* is located near the mound. The ceramic industries found are OCP, NBP, K, EM and LM.

Khandasa: The village lies on latitude $81^{0}47'$ N and longitude $26^{0}36'$ E. It lies 9 km to the east of the P.S. The mound lies at a distance of 0.8 km to the south of village. The area of the mound is 03 acre. Height of the mound is 5 meter. *Kotwa Budhwa Baba* place lies on the mound. The ceramic industry found is OCP.

Khurdana: The village lies on latitude $81^{0}53'10''$ N and longitude $26^{0}42'30''$ E. The area of the mound is 0.6 acre. The ceramic industry found is OCP and Late Chalcolithic.

Kotdeeh: The village lies on latitude $81^{0}53'30''$ N and longitude $26^{0}41'10''$ E. It lies 14 km of the P.S. The mound lies in the middle of the village. The area of the mound is 0.4 acre. Height of the mound is plain. The ceramic industries found are OCP, G and EM.

Kotiya: The village lies on latitude 81⁰45′30″ N and longitude 26⁰37′40″ E. It lies 4 km to the north of the P.S. The mound lies at a distance of 2 km to the north of village. The area of the mound is 0.4 acre. Height of the mound is 3.3 meter. The ceramic industries found are NBP, K, EM and LM.

Kunjai ka Purwa: The village lies on latitude 81⁰45′30″ N and longitude 26⁰37′40″ E. It lies 12 km from the P.S. The area of the mound is 0.2 acre. The ceramic industries found are NBP and K.

Nagipur: The village lies on latitude 81⁰46′30″ N and longitude 26⁰35′50″ E. It lies 9 km to the south of the P.S. The mound lies at a distance of 2.5 km to the south of village. The area of the mound is 6 acre. Height of the mound is 2.6 meter. The place of *Murtian Bhawani* is located on the mound. The ceramic industry found is LM.

Narsada: The village lies on latitude 81⁰50′ N and longitude 26⁰37′10″ E. It lies 10 km to the east of the P.S. The mound lies at a distance of 0.2 km to the east of village. The area of the mound is 2 acre. Height of the mound is 3.3 meter. The bricks of sizes 7x5x2.5 and 9x6x2.5 inch are found on the mound. *Mahadewan Mandir* is located on the mound. The ceramic industry found is LM.

Navgawa (Manudeeh): The village lies on latitude 81⁰49′30″ N and longitude 26⁰37′50″ E. It lies 7 km to the north-east of the P.S. The mound lies at a distance of 0.2 km to the south-west of village. The area of the mound is 6 acre. Height of the mound is 1.6 meter. *Karaudhi Taal* is located near the mound. The ceramic industry found is LM.

Orwa: The village lies on latitude 81⁰47′10″ N and longitude 26⁰40′20″ E. It lies 4 km to the north of the P.S. The mound lies at a distance of 0.1 km to the north of village. The area of the mound is 5 acre. Height of the mound is 5 meter. The bricks of sizes 8x7x1/2 and 7x4x2 inch and four wells are found on the mound. *Ujagir Baba Mandir* is located on the mound. The ceramic industry found is LM.

Shatrughan ka Purwa: The village lies on latitude 81⁰47′ N and longitude 26⁰36′40″ E. It lies 5 km to the south-east of the P.S. The mound lies at a distance of 0.5 km to the north of village. The area of the mound is 3 acre. Height of the mound is 1.3 meter. The ceramic industries found are OCP, K, G and EM.

Sirsid: The village lies on latitude 81⁰52′10″ N and longitude 26⁰3′25″ E. It lies 11 km to the south of the P.S. The mound lies at a distance of 0.1 km to the north of village. The area of the mound is 1 acre. Height of the mound is 5 meter. *Kabrsitan* and *Shiva Mandir* is located on the mound. The ceramic industry found is OCP. This mound is ascribed to *Bhars*[20].

Taal Dholi: The village lies on latitude N and longitude E. It lies 10 km from the P.S. The mound lies at a distance of 1 km to the north of village. The area of the mound is 10 acre. Height of the mound is 1.6 meter. *Deehawa Baba* place is located on the mound. The ceramic industries found are OCP, K and LM.

Tiktee: The village lies on latitude 81⁰45′40″ N and longitude 26⁰34′45″ E. It lies 12 km from the P.S. The area of the mound is 10.4 acre. Height of the mound is 1.3 meter. The ceramic industry found is OCP.

Vinayakpur: The village lies on latitude 81°47′20″ N and longitude 26°40′ E. It lies 1 km from the P.S. The mound lies to the east of the village. The area of the mound is 10.4 acre. The ceramic industries found are EM, Late Chalcolithic and TC pieces.

P.S. Mawai District Ayodhya

Baba ka Purwa: The village lies on latitude 81°41′15″ N and longitude 26°35′30″ E. The area of the mound is 10.2 acre. Height of the mound is 5 meter. The bricks of sizes 9x9x3 inch are found on the mound. The ceramic industries found are NBP, K, EM and LM.

Bagheri (Phirojpur): The village lies on latitude 81°37′15″ N and longitude 26°42′15″ E. It lies 12 km to the east of the P.S. The mound lies to the east of the village. The area of the mound is 4 acre. Height of the mound is 2.4 meter. River *Kalyani* flows near the mound. *Budhe Baba Ramdas (Pakara Haar) ka Sthan* is located on the mound. The ceramic industry found is LM.

Bahbara purwa: The village lies on latitude 81°41′15″ N and longitude 26°36′45″ E. It lies 27 km to the south-east of the P.S. The mound lies at a distance of 0.2 km to the south of river *Gomti*. *Raja Dhobi ka Kot* is located on the mound. The ceramic industries found are OCP and NBP.

Bartara: The village lies on latitude 81°37′ N and longitude 26°45′50″ E. It lies 7 km to the east of the P.S. The mound lies at a distance of 0.3 km to the east of village. The area of the mound is 5 acre. Height of the mound is 0.9 meter. River *Tamsa* flows near the mound. The bricks of sizes 6x5x1.5 and 6x4.5x1 inch are found on the mound. *Dhobi Ghat* and *Kabristan* are located on the mound. The ceramic industry found is LM.

Basaudhi: The village lies on latitude 81°37′20″ N and longitude 26°46′20″ E. It lies 5 km to the south of the P.S. The area of the mound is 4 acre. Height of the mound is 2 meter. *Bheet* and *Jhakra Talaab* is located on the mound. The ceramic industries found are OCP, NBP and LM.

Bhanipur: The village lies on latitude N and longitude E. It lies 16 km to the north-west of the P.S. The mound lies at a distance of 0.3 km to the west of the village. The area of the mound is 20 acre. Height of the mound is 1.6 meter. *Bheet* and *Jhakra Talaab* are located on and near the mound respectively. The ceramic industries found are OCP, NBP and LM.

Bihara Mauja (mound 1): The village lies on latitude 81°43′15″ N and longitude 26°36′10″ E. It lies 42 km to the east of the P.S. The mound lies at a distance of 0.5 km to the north of village. The area of the mound is 6 acre. Height of the mound is 4.5 meter. The bricks of sizes 10x7x2.5 and 9x7x2.5 inch are found on the mound. *Hans Giri Baba ki Kuti* is located on the mound. The ceramic industry found is EM.

Bihara Mauja (mound 2): The village lies on latitude 81°41′15″ N and longitude 26°35′50″ E. It lies to the south-east of the P.S. The area of the mound is 3.2 acre. Height of the mound is 2.6 meter. The bricks of sizes 2x3x1 inch are found on the mound. The ceramic industries found are NP, K, G, EM, LM and Gupta T.C.

Bihara Mauja (mound 3): The village lies on latitude 81°43′15″ N and longitude 26°36′10″ E. It lies 42 km to the east of the P.S. The mound lies at a distance of 0.5 km to the north of village. The area of the mound is 6 acre. Height of the mound is 4.5 meter. The bricks of sizes 9x8x3 and 8x6x2 inch are found on the mound. *Akhaini Talaab* and *Bheetawa* are located near and on the mound respectively. The ceramic industries found are K and G.

Bihara (Primary School): The village lies on latitude 81°41′15″ N and longitude 26°35′50″ E. It lies to the south-east of the P.S. The area of the mound is 2 acre. Height of the mound is 5 meter. The bricks of sizes 9x7x2 inch are found on the mound. *Bheetawa* is located on the mound. The ceramic industry found is EM.

Chhoti Bani: The village lies on latitude 81°38′30″ N and longitude 26°39′45″ E. The area of the mound is 3 acre. Height of the mound is 4.6 meter. *Mehedi Veer Baba ka Sthan* is located on the mound. The ceramic industries found are OCP, NBP and K.

Dullapur (Mawai Crossing): The village lies on latitude 81°36′30″ N and longitude 26°46′30″ E. It lies 05 km to the north of the P.S. The mound lies to the east of the village. The area of the mound is 1 acre. Height of the mound is plain. *Talaab* is located near the mound. The ceramic industry found is LM.

Dwarikapur: The village lies on latitude 81°37′ N and longitude 26°41′45″ E. It lies 10 km to the south-east of the P.S. The mound lies at a distance of 0.3 km to the east of village. The area of the mound is 4.1 acre. Height of the mound is 5.4 meter. The highest portion of the mound is called *Unchwa*. The ceramic industry found is LM.

Dwarikapur: The village lies on latitude 81°37′ N and longitude 26°42′ E. It lies 15 km to the south of the P.S. The mound lies at a distance of 0.1 km to the west of river *Kalyani*. The area of the mound is 10 acre. Height of the mound is 10 meter. *Dwarika Bhartiya Mandir* is located on the mound. The ceramic industry found is LM.

Ganeshpur: The village lies on latitude 81°44′30″ N and longitude 20°37′15″ E. The mound lies at a distance of 0.2 km to the east of the River *Gomti*. The area of the mound is 04 acre. Height of the mound is 10 meter. *Siktaha Kotawa* is located on the mound. The ceramic industries found are OCP, Late Chalcolithic (of corded ware tradition), NBP, EM and LM.

Hansrajpur: The village lies on latitude 81°34′ N and longitude 26°40′10″ E. It lies 31 km to the south-east of the P.S. The mound lies at a distance of 0.8 km to the west of village. The area of the mound is 5 acre. Height of the mound is 3 meter. *Bisahi* and *Mahadeva* places are located on the mound. The ceramic industry found is LM.

Itaha Mauja Sunba: The village lies on latitude 81°41′30″ N and longitude 26°36′50″ E. The area of the mound is 1 acre. Height of the mound is 1.6 meter. *Tanduliya Nala* is located near the mound. The ceramic industries found are OCP, NBP and K.

Jia ka Purwa: The village lies on latitude 81°37′20″ N and longitude 26°41′28″ E. It lies 12 km to the north-west of the P.S. The mound lies at a distance of 0.3 km to the south-east of the confluence of the river *Kalyani* and *Gomti*. The area of the mound is 20 acre. Height of the mound is 31 meter. *Tikta ka Raja* is located on the mound. The ceramic industries found are OCP, Late Chalcolithic, NBP and LM.

Kaithi Ghat ka Purwa (Majra Hansrajpur): The village lies on latitude 81°34′ N and longitude 26°40′10″ E. It lies 34 km to the south from the P.S. The mound lies at a distance of 0.8 km to the west of village. The area of the mound is 2 acre. Height of the mound is 2.4 meter. River *Gomti* lies near the mound. *Mehendi ke Khet* and *Kali Mata ka Sthan* are located on the mound. The ceramic industry found is LM.

Karaudi (Mauja Saidpur): The village lies on latitude 81°43′15″ N and longitude 26°26′30″ E. It lies 28 km to the east of the P.S. The mound lies at a distance of 0.5 km to the south of village. The area of the mound is 1.4 acre. Height of the mound is 6.3 meter. *Bheetawa* and *Kotawa* are located on the mound. The ceramic industry found is LM.

Karauli: The village lies on latitude 81°39′ N and longitude 26°45′30″ E. It lies 10 km to the north-east of the P.S. The area of the mound is 6.6 acre. Height of the mound is 7.3 meter. The ceramic industry found is LM.

Kasaripur (Madar ka Purwa): The village lies on latitude 81°40′ N and longitude 26°35′50″ E. It lies to the south-east of the P.S. The area of the mound is 06 acre. Height of the mound is 8.3 meter. The place of *Biran Baba* is located on the mound. The ceramic industries found are NBP and K.

Kasari (Madkiyan Purwa): The village lies on latitude 81°40′45″ N and longitude 26°35′45″ E. It lies to the south-east of the P.S. The area of the mound is 10 acre. Height of the mound is 13.3 meter. The place called *Sitkaha* is located on the mound. The ceramic industry found is LM.

Khandawa: The village lies on latitude 81°37′30″ N and longitude 26°43′ E. It lies 12 km to the east of the P.S. The mound lies to the east of the village. The area of the mound is 20 acre. Height of the mound is 1.2 meter. The bricks of sizes 9x6x2, 9x6x2.5, 7x6x2 and 6x4.5x1 inch are found on the mound. *Rauza Baba ka Sthan* is located on the mound. The ceramic industry found is LM.

Koili ka Purwa (Mauja Saidpur): The village lies on latitude 81°44′20″ N and longitude 26°37′44″ E. It lies 34 km to the east of the P.S. The mound lies at a distance of 0.8 km to the east of village. The area of the mound is 06 acre. Height of the mound is 3.6 meter. The ceramic industry found is LM.

Kotawa: The village lies on latitude 81°37′30″ N and longitude 26°43′45″ E. It lies 06 km to the east of the P.S. The mound lies at a distance of 1 km to the south of village. The area of the mound is 05 acre. Height of the mound is 9.5 meter. *Hanuman ji ki Kutiya* and *Hanuman Gufa* are located on the mound. The ceramic industry found is LM.

Kudara: The village lies on latitude 81°39′20″ N and longitude 26°43′10″ E. It lies 16 km to the east of the P.S. The mound lies at a distance of 0.5 km to the west of village. The area of the mound is 5 acre. Height of the mound is 3 meter. The bricks of sizes 7x5x2.5 inch are found on the mound. *Durga Mata Mandir* and *Chandi Baba ka Sthan* are located on the mound. The ceramic industry found is LM.

Kusahari: The village lies on latitude 81°34′ N and longitude 26°46′45″ E. It lies 7 km to the west of the P.S. The mound lies at a distance of 0.3 km to the west of village. The area of the mound is 10 acre. Height of the mound is 9 meter. River *Kalyani* lies near the mound. The bricks of sizes 10x7x2 inch are found on the mound. *Tekara* and *Laukhari Masjid* are located on the mound. The ceramic industry found is LM.

Lakhnipur: The village lies on latitude 81°38′ N and longitude 26°46′ E. It lies 10 km to the north-west of the P.S. The area of the mound is 5 acre. Height of the mound is 1.3 meter. *Deehariya Haar* is located on the mound. The ceramic industries found are OCP, Late Chalcolithic (of corded ware tradition), NBP, K and LM.

Manipur: The village lies on latitude 81°36′10″ N and longitude 26°47′20″ E. It lies 16 km to the north-west of the P.S. The area of the mound is 2 acre. Height of the mound is 1.6 meter. *Chak Kotawa Baba ki Kuti* is located on the mound. The ceramic industry found is LM.

Matya Newada: The village lies on latitude 81°40′ N and longitude 26°40′10″ E. It lies 20 km to the east of the P.S. The area of the mound is 3 acre. Height of the mound is 1 meter. *Gosai Baba ka Sthan* is located on the mound. The ceramic industries found are OCP, NBP, K and LM.

Mawai (mound 1): The village lies on latitude 81°36′ N and longitude 26°44′36″ E. It lies 2 km to the south of the P.S. The mound lies at a distance of 0.2 km to the south-east of the river *Kalyani*. The area of the mound is 10 acre. Height of the mound is 10 meter. *Peer Baba ka Sthan* is located on the mound. The ceramic industry found is LM.

Mawai (mound 2): The village lies on latitude 81°36′ N and longitude 26°44′30″ E. It lies 2 km to the north of the P.S. The mound lies at a distance of 1 km to the north of village. The area of the mound is 4 acre. Height of the mound is 3 meter. *Dhobin Baghiya* is located on the mound. The ceramic industry found is LM.

Mawai Bazar: The village lies on latitude 81°36′ N and longitude 26°44′30′ E. It lies ½ km to the south of the P.S. The mound lies at a distance of 0.6 km to the south of village. The area of the mound is 07 acre. Height of the mound is 12 meter. The bricks of sizes 7x4.5x1.5 inch are found on the mound. A tomb called *Makbara* is located on the mound. The ceramic industry found is LM.

Maya Purwa (Majra Arauli): The village lies on latitude 81°40′50″ N and longitude 26°44′ E. It lies 16 km to the north-east of the P.S. The mound lies at a distance of 0.05 km to the north-east of village. The area of the mound is 4 acre. Height of the mound is 3 meter. The bricks of sizes 8x6x2 inch are found on the mound. *Bheetawa Talaab* is located on the mound. The ceramic industry found is LM.

Medai Gosai ka Purwa: The village lies on latitude 81°40′ N and longitude 26°36′50″ E. It lies 22 km to the south-east of the P.S. The mound lies at a distance of 0.2 km to the north of the village. The area of the mound is 80 acre. Height of the mound is 5 meter. *Betawa Nala* is located near the mound. The ceramic industries found are EM and LM.

Mohammadpur Dawad: The village lies on latitude 81°37′ N and longitude 26°45′50″ E. It lies 7 km to the south-west of the P.S. The area of the mound is 3 acre. Height of the mound is 1.3 meter. A place called *Kaulaha* is located on the mound. The ceramic industries found are OCP, BS and NBP.

Narauli: The village lies on latitude 81⁰40′15″ N and longitude 26⁰44′20″ E. It lies 16 km to the east of the P.S. The mound lies at a distance of 0.5 km to the north of village. The area of the mound is 4 acre. Height of the mound is plain. The bricks of sizes 9x5x1.5 inch are found on the mound. *Shatnami Vidyapeeth Inter College* is located on the mound. The ceramic industry found is LM.

Navgawa Deeh: The village lies on latitude 81⁰35′ N and longitude 26⁰40′45″ E. It lies 20 km to the north of the P.S. The mound lies to the north of the river *Gomti*. The area of the mound is 4.4 acre. Height of the mound is 15 meter. *Shri Mahapurush Mandir* is located on the mound. The ceramic industries found are OCP, NBP and K.

Naya Purwa (Majra Rechh): The village lies on latitude 81⁰37′ N and longitude 26⁰28′10′ E. It lies 23 km to the east of the P.S. The mound lies to the east of the village. The area of the mound is 10 acre. Height of the mound is 5.4 meter. River *Gomti* flows near the mound. The bricks of sizes 9x7x2 inch are found on the mound. *Ituwa* and *Deehawa* are located on the mound. The ceramic industries found are EM and LM.

Neora: The village lies on latitude 81⁰38′20″ N and longitude 26⁰43′30″ E. It lies 11 km to the south-east of the P.S. The mound lies at a distance of 0.2 km to the south of village. The area of the mound is 25 acre. Height of the mound is 3.6 meter. River *Kalyani* flows near the mound. *Tikuri* is located on the mound. The ceramic industry found is LM.

Newara: The village lies on latitude 81⁰38′20″ N and longitude 26⁰43′30″ E. It lies 8 km to the east of the P.S. The mound lies at a distance of 2 km to the west of river *Kalyani*. The area of the mound is 30 acre. Height of the mound is 4 meter. *Tikuri, Bheet* and *Jhakra Talaab* are located near the mound. The ceramic industry found is LM.

Ohramau-Sahjanwa: The village lies on latitude 81⁰36′30″ N and longitude 26⁰43′ E. It lies 6 km to the north-west of the P.S. The area of the mound is 1 acre. Height of the mound is 10 meter. The mound lies at a distance of near river *Kalyani*. *Imli Veer Baba ka Mandir* is located on the mound. The ceramic industries found are NBP and K.

Pakariya: The village lies on latitude 81⁰41′30″ N and longitude 26⁰43′30″ E. It lies 17 km to the east of the P.S. The mound lies at a distance of 0.6 km to the north-west of village. The area of the mound is 0.8 acre. Height of the mound is 1.2 meter. The bricks of sizes 9x6x2 inch are found on the mound. *Saraha Baghiya* and *Lala ki Samadhi* are located on the mound. The ceramic industry found is LM.

Pragdutt purwa (Mauja Ratan Purwa): The village lies on latitude 81⁰37′ N and longitude 26⁰40′50″ E. It lies 12 km to the south-east of the P.S. The mound lies at a distance of 0.4 km to the north of village. The area of the mound is 1 acre. Height of the mound is 2.10 meter. River *Gomti* flows near the mound. *Sherwa Bhati* place is located on the mound. The ceramic industry found is LM.

Pure Baiju Pande ka Purwa (Majra Saidpur): The village lies on latitude 81⁰43′15″ N and longitude 26⁰37′15″ E. It lies 35 km to the east of the P.S. The mound lies to the west of the village. The area of the mound is 5 acre. Height of the mound is 1.5 meter. The ceramic industry found is LM.

Ramdeeha: The village lies on latitude 81°37′20″ N and longitude 26°39′20″ E. It lies 22 km to the south-east of the P.S. The mound lies to the south from the village. The area of the mound is 0.4 acre. Height of the mound is 1.8 meter. *Dhanu ka Talaab* is located near the mound. The ceramic industry found is LM.

Rechh: The village lies on latitude 81°37′ N and longitude 26°38′10″ E. It lies 27 km to the east of the P.S. The mound lies at a distance of 0.2 km to the west of village. The area of the mound is 20 acre. Height of the mound is 4.2 meter. River *Gomti* flows near the mound. *Shiva Mandir* and *Baba Kakori Das ki Kuti* are located on the mound. The ceramic industry found is LM.

Sadwa: The village lies on latitude 81°38′30″ N and longitude 26°43′ E. It lies to the east of the P.S. The area of the mound is 14 acre. Height of the mound is plain. *Mazar* and *Kabristan* are located on the mound. The ceramic industry found is LM.

Saidpur: The village lies on latitude 81°45′30″ N and longitude 26°37′50″ E. The area of the mound is 10 acre. Height of the mound is 2.3 meter. The ceramic industries found are OCP, NBP, K, EM and LM.

Sandwa: The village lies on latitude 81°38′30″ N and longitude 26°43′10″ E. It lies 12 km to the east of the P.S. The mound lies to the east of the village. The area of the mound is 20 acre. Height of the mound is 1.2 meter. The bricks of sizes 9x6x2, 9x6x2, 7x6x2 and 6x4.5x1 inch are found on the mound. The tomb called *Shaheed Mard Shah @ Rauza Baba ka Sthan* is located on the mound. The ceramic industries found are EM and LM.

Sherpur: The village lies on latitude 81°37′ N and longitude 26°41′40″ E. It lies 8 km to the west of the P.S. The mound lies at a distance of 0.8 km to the north of village. The area of the mound is 4 acre. Height of the mound is 2.10 meter. The ceramic industry found is LM.

Sherpur Jangal: The village lies on latitude 81°37′ N and longitude 26°41′45″ E. It lies 8 km to the west of the P.S. The mound lies at a distance of 1 km to the north-west of river *Kalyani*. The area of the mound is 2 acre. Height of the mound is 2.3 meter. *Semraha Nala* is located near the mound. The ceramic industries found are OCP and NBP.

Sipahiya: The village lies on latitude 81°36′15″ N and longitude 26°44′15″ E. It lies 2 km to the east from the P.S. The mound lies at a distance of 0.5 km to the east of village. The area of the mound is 5 acre. Height of the mound is 8.1 meter. *Jharna Nala* and *Tikuri* are located near and on the mound respectively. The ceramic industry found is LM.

Sunba: The village lies on latitude 81°41′15″ N and longitude 26°37′ E. It lies 43 km to the south-east of the P.S. The mound lies at a distance of 0.2 km to the east of village. The area of the mound is 5 acre. Height of the mound is 3.6 meter. River *Gomti* flows near the mound. *Pakara* and *Navara* are located on the mound. The ceramic industry found is LM.

Taalgaon: The village lies on latitude 81°39′ N and longitude 26°41′40″ E. It lies 15 km to the east of the P.S. The mound lies at a distance of 0.1 km to the north-west of village. The area of the mound is 1 acre.

Height of the mound is 1.5 meter. *Bheetawa Karbala* is located on the mound. The ceramic industry found is LM.

Takiya ka Purwa: The village lies on latitude 81⁰33′45″ N and longitude 26⁰46′45″ E. It lies 10 km to the north of the P.S. The mound lies at a distance of 0.3 km to the west of river *Kalyani*. The area of the mound is 10 acre. Height of the mound is 6.6 meter. *Tikra* is located on the mound. The ceramic industries found are OCP and Late Chalcolithic.

Umapur: The village lies on latitude 81⁰38′30″ N and longitude 26⁰39′30″ E. It lies 25 km to the east of the P.S. The mound lies to the south of the village. The area of the mound is 2 acre. Height of the mound is 1.2 meter. *Sri Baba Neval Das ki Samadhi* is located on the mound. The ceramic industry found is LM.

P.S. Patranga District Ayodhya

Ashrafpur: The village lies on latitude 81^{0}34′40″ N and longitude 26^{0}47′45″ E. It lies 10 km to the north-east of the P.S. The mound lies to the south of the river *Kalyani*. The area of the mound is 4.4 acre. Height of the mound is 07 meter. The ceramic industries found are OCP, K, G, EM and LM.

Ashrafpur Gangrela: The village lies on latitude 81^{0}34′36″ N and longitude 26^{0}47′45″ E. It lies 7 km to the south of the P.S. The area of the mound is 3.6 acre. Height of the mound is 3.3 meter. The bricks are strewn on the mound. The ceramic industry found is LM.

Avghawan Nagar: The village lies on latitude 81^{0}39′ N and longitude 26^{0}47′50″ E. It lies 7 km to the west of the P.S. The mound lies at a distance of 0.5 km to the west of village. The area of the mound is 10 acre. *Balika Inter College* is located on the mound. The ceramic industry found is LM.

Bajauli: The village lies on latitude 81^{0}42′ N and longitude 26^{0}46′10″ E. It lies 8 km to the north of the P.S. The mound lies at a distance of 0.1 km to the north-east of *Meel ka Nala*. The area of the mound is 1.6 acre. *Bargadiya ka Talaab* is located near the mound. The ceramic industry found is LM.

Basaudhi: The village lies on latitude 81^{0}37′20″ N and longitude 26^{0}46′15″ E. It lies 8 km to the north-east of the P.S. The area of the mound is 5 acre. Height of the mound is 1.6 meter. *Tanai Chak* is located on the mound. The ceramic industries found are K, G, EM and LM.

Deewali: The village lies on latitude 81^{0}41′20″ N and longitude 26^{0}48′50″ E. It lies 8 km to the south-west of the P.S. The area of the mound is 6 acre. Height of the mound is 1.6 meter. The bricks of sizes 6x5x3.5 inch are found on the mound. *Sitakiha* and *Khajuha* Lake are located on and near the mound respectively. The ceramic industries found are OCP and NBP.

Dilwai: The village lies on latitude 81^{0}39′ N and longitude 26^{0}46′20″ E. It lies 6 km to the south-east of the P.S. The mound lies at a distance of 0.8 km to the north of village. The area of the mound is 4 acre. The bricks of sizes 9x6x2 inch are found on the mound. *Shri Kunjal Das Giri Baba ki Kutiya* is located on the mound. The ceramic industry found is LM.

Ghosawal: The village lies on latitude 81^{0}36′30″ N and longitude 26^{0}49′ E. It lies 3 km to the south of the P.S. The area of the mound is 4 acre. Height of the mound is 1.3 meter. Place of *Aholiya Baba Shaheed* and 3 wells are also located on the mound. The ceramic industry found is LM.

Gurenda: The village lies on latitude 81^{0}41′45″ N and longitude 26^{0}40′50″ E. It lies 8 km to the south-west of the P.S. The mound lies at a distance of 3 km to the east of *Khajura* Lake. The area of the mound is 30 acre. Height of the mound is 4 meter. The ceramic industries found are OCP, K, G, EM and LM.

Ichauliya: The village lies on latitude 81^{0}42′15″ N and longitude 26^{0}48′45″ E. It lies 8 km to the north-east of the P.S. The area of the mound is 5 acre. Height of the mound is 1.3 meter. *Chandi* Lake is located near the mound. The ceramic industries found are OCP, NBP and K.

Jakhauli: The village lies on latitude 81^{0}40′ N and longitude 26^{0}48′45″ E. It lies 4 km to the south-west of the P.S. The area of the mound is 14 acre. *Bheetawa* is located on the mound and a railway track cuts across the same. The ceramic industries found are OCP, EM and LM.

Jarayan Kala: The village lies on latitude 81^{0}38′45″ N and longitude 26^{0}47′15″ E. It lies 5 km to the north-west of the P.S. *Babai ka Matha* and *Bare Tara Jheel* are located on and near the mound respectively. The ceramic industries found are OCP and NBP. This mound is ascribed to *Bhars*[21].

Kashiram ka Purwa/ Bargadi: The village lies on latitude 81^{0}40′ N and longitude 26^{0}48′40″ E. It lies 4 km to the south-west of the P.S. The area of the mound is 5 acre. *Paasi Talla Tank* is located near the mound. The ceramic industries found are OCP, NBP and LM.

Khurdaha: The village lies on latitude 81^{0}42′15″ N and longitude 26^{0}48′45″ E. It lies 6 km to the south-west of the P.S. The area of the mound is 3 acre. The bricks of sizes 6x3x4 inch and five wells are found on the mound. *Katra Talaab* and *Kabristan* are located near and on the mound respectively. The ceramic industry found is OCP.

Kopepur: The village lies on latitude 81^{0}44′30″ N and longitude 26^{0}50′40″ E. It lies 20 km to the east of the P.S. The area of the mound is 12 acre. Height of the mound is 1.6 meter. *Kali Mataji ka Chaura* is located on the mound. The ceramic industries found are OCP, K, G and LM.

Makhdoompur: The village lies on latitude 81^{0}38′ N and longitude 26^{0}49′10″ E. It lies 3 km to the north of the P.S. The mound lies at a distance of 0.5 km to the south of *Sharda Sahayak* Canal and *Sherapar Talaab*. *Sherapar ka Bheet* is located on the mound. The ceramic industries found are OCP and LM.

Manapur: The village lies on latitude 81^{0}30′10″ N and longitude 26^{0}47′20″ E. It lies 5 km to the north of the P.S. The mound lies at a distance of 0.6 km to the west of *Sharda Sahayak* Canal. The area of the mound is 4 acre. The height of the mound is 1.6 meter. The bricks of sizes 6x5x3.5 inch are found on the mound. *Babai ka Matha* and *Bare Tara Jheel* are located on and near the mound respectively. The ceramic industries found are OCP, NBP, K, G and LM.

Maqdoompur: The village lies on latitude 81^{0}38′ N and longitude 26^{0}49′10″ E. It lies 1.5 km to the south of the P.S. The mound lies to the east of the village. The area of the mound is 2 acre. Height of the mound is 1.2 meter. The ceramic industry found is LM.

Mia ka Purwa (Majra Jarayal Kala): The village lies on latitude 81^{0}38′45″ N and longitude 26^{0}47′15″ E. It lies 9 km to the south of the P.S. The area of the mound is 6 acre. *Bara Talaab* and *Kabristan* are located near and on the mound respectively. The ceramic industries found are OCP and NBP.

Nagra: The village lies on latitude 81^{0}36′50″ N and longitude 26^{0}49′20″ E. It lies 2 km to the east of the P.S. The area of the mound is 4 acre. Height of the mound is 1.6 meter. *Banjaran ka Dera* is located on the mound. The ceramic industries found are OCP and NBP.

Patranga: The village lies on latitude 81^{0}36′ N and longitude 26^{0}50′40″ E. It lies to the east of the P.S. The mound lies at a distance of 0.4 km to the north of village. The area of the mound is 5 acre. Height of the mound is 0.9 meter. The bricks of sizes 7x5x1 and 6x5x1 inch are found on the mound. *Rani ka*

Talaab and *Shiva Mandir* are located near and on the mound respectively. The ceramic industry found is LM.

Patranga: The village lies on latitude 81°36′ N and longitude 26°50′30″ E. It lies 2 km to the north-west of the P.S. The area of the mound is 4 acre. The ceramic industries found are OCP and NBP.

Purai: The village lies on latitude 81°40′20″ N and longitude 26°45′40″ E. It lies 10 km to the north-west of the P.S. The area of the mound is 4 acre. The height of the mound is 2.6 meter. *Itiya Shaheed Baba ka Sthan* is located on the mound. The ceramic industries found are OCP, NBP, K, EM and LM.

Raja Khan ka Purwa: The village lies on latitude 81°41′ N and longitude 26°45′45″ E. It lies 15 km to the north-west of the P.S. The area of the mound is 3.6 acre. Height of the mound is 2.6 meter. The ceramic industries found are OCP, K and LM.

Rajja Nagar: The village lies on latitude 81°39′ N and longitude 26°47′ E. It lies 9 km to the south-east of the P.S. The mound lies at a distance of 0.1 km to the north of village. The area of the mound is 5 acre. Height of the mound is 1.2 meter. *Bheetawa* is located on the mound. The ceramic industry found is LM.

Rani Mau: The village lies on latitude 81°35′15″ N and longitude 26°47′30″ E. It lies 7 km to the south of the P.S. The area of the mound is 3.6 acre. Height of the mound is 3.3 meter. Mound is called *Rani ka Kot*. The ceramic industries found are OCP, NBP and K.

Sahabad Chak (Natwan Dera): The village lies on latitude 81°39′ N and longitude 26°47′45″ E. It lies 9 km to the north-west of the P.S. The area of the mound is 2.4 acre. Height of the mound is 1.3 meter. *Bara Talaab* is located near the mound. The ceramic industries found are OCP, NBP, K and LM.

Saretha: The village lies on latitude 81°41′ N and longitude 26°45′45″ E. It lies 12 km to the south-west of the P.S. The area of the mound is 1.8 acre. Height of the mound is 1.6 meter. *Bheet* and shrine of *Shri Baba Kharcha Dev* are located on the mound. The ceramic industry found is rude handmade OCP, NBP, K, EM and LM.

Sulemanpur (Naktadeeh): The village lies on latitude 81°41′30″ N and longitude 26°48′15″ E. It lies 10 km to the south-east of the P.S. The mound lies to the south of the village. The area of the mound is 30 acre. The ceramic industry found is LM.

Sulemanpur (Sitkahiya): The village lies on latitude 81°41′30″ N and longitude 26°48′15″ E. It lies 10 km to the south-east of the P.S. The mound lies at a distance of 0.7 km to the east of village. The area of the mound is 3 acre. The ceramic industry found is LM.

Sultanpur: The village lies on latitude 81°35′15″ N and longitude 26°49′20″ E. It lies 8 km to the west of the P.S. The mound lies at a distance of 1 km to the north of village. The area of the mound is 6 acre. Height of the mound is 4.2 meter. River *Kalyani* flows near the mound. *Itahuwa* and *Babaji ki Kuti* are located on the mound. The ceramic industry found is LM.

P.S. Rudauli District Ayodhya

Aeithar: The village lies on latitude 81^{0}45′20″ N and longitude 26^{0}49′50″ E. It lies 12 km to the north of the P.S. The mound lies to the west of the village. The area of the mound is 1 acre. Height of the mound is 2.3 meter. *Deeh har* is located on the mound. The ceramic industries found are OCP, NBP and K.

Ahiran Purwa: The village lies on latitude 81^{0}50′45″ N and longitude 26^{0}42′ E. It lies 5 km to the north-east of the P.S. The area of the mound is 10 acre. Height of the mound is 4 meter. *Kariya Bhole Baba, Dheepwa* and *Sankata Devi Mandir* are located on the mound. The ceramic industry found is LM.

Ahlana: The village lies on latitude 81^{0}43′45″ N and longitude 26^{0}39′10″ E. It lies 8 km to the south of the P.S. The area of the mound is 5 acre. Height of the mound is 2.3 meter. *Aadam Shaheed Baba ka Sthan* is located on the mound. The ceramic industries found are EM and LM.

Aihat @ Ehar: The village lies on latitude 81^{0}48′ N and longitude 26^{0}42′45″ E. It lies 7 km to the east of the P.S. The mound lies at a distance of 0.3 km to the south-west of village. The area of the mound is 7 acre. Height of the mound is 2.10 meter. The bricks of sizes 5x6x2.5 inch are found on the mound. *Kakrahi* and a Lake is located on and near the mound respectively. The ceramic industry found is LM.

Baari: The village lies on latitude 81^{0}46′45″ N and longitude 26^{0}42′ E. It lies 12 km to the south-east of the P.S. *Jharokhar sthan* is located on the mound. The ceramic industry found is LM.

Bichala: The village lies on latitude 81^{0}46′ N and longitude 26^{0}48′40″ E. It lies 8 km to the north of the P.S. The mound lies at a distance of 0.4 km to the south of village. The area of the mound is ½ acre. *Shiva Mandir* and *Prathmik Vidyalaya* are located on the mound. The ceramic industry found is LM.

Bidhar: The village lies on latitude 81^{0}46′20″ N and longitude 24^{0}42′40″ E. It lies 4 km to the south-east of the P.S. The mound lies at a distance of 0.2 km to the west of village. The area of the mound is 5 acre. Height of the mound is 1.2 meter. *Hanuman Garhi* and *Gulam Shah Baba ka Sthan* is located on the mound. The ceramic industry found is LM.

Dashrath Mau: The village lies on latitude 81^{0}44′30″ N and longitude 26^{0}49′ E. It lies 9 km to the north of the P.S. The mound lies at a distance of 0.3 km to the north of village. The area of the mound is 5 acre. Height of the mound is 1.8 meter. The ceramic industry found is LM.

Deokali: The village lies on latitude 81^{0}45′30″ N and longitude 26^{0}47′40″ E. It lies 10 km to the north-east of the P.S. The area of the mound is 1 acre. *Deokali Mandir* is located on the mound. The ceramic industry found is LM.

Dheepawa Purwa (Teekar): The village lies on latitude 81^{0}43′ N and longitude 26^{0}45′15″ E. It lies 5 km to the east of the P.S. The mound lies to the west of village. The area of the mound is 4 acre. *Shaheed Chaudhary's* shrine is located on the mound. The ceramic industries found are OCP, Late Chalcolithic (of corded tradition), NBP and K.

Duddhadhari: The village lies on latitude 81^{0}44′30″ N and longitude 26^{0}45′40″ E. It lies 1 km to the north of the P.S. The mound lies at a distance of 0.2 km to the west of village. The area of the mound is

08 acre. Height of the mound is 1.8 meter. *Bari* and *Chhoti Duddhadhari Masjid* are located on the mound. The ceramic industry found is LM.

Ferozpur Maqdumi: The village lies on latitude 81⁰43′30″ N and longitude 26⁰42′30″ E. It lies 6 km to the south of the P.S. The mound lies at a distance of 1 km to the north of village. The area of the mound is 6.6 acre. Height of the mound is 1 meter. *Chakra ka Siwan* and *Nivera Talaab* are located on and near the mound respectively. The ceramic industry found is OCP.

Gauriya Mau: The village lies on latitude 82⁰48′30″ N and longitude 26⁰45′20″ E. It lies 6 km to the north-west of the P.S. The mound lies at a distance of 0.5 km to the east of village. The area of the mound is 1 acre. *Shishain Bagiya (Nara)* is located on the mound. The ceramic industries found are OCP and Middle Chalcolithic (of corded ware tradition).

Gogawan: The village lies on latitude 81⁰43′ N and longitude 26⁰42′15″ E. It lies 2 km to the west of the P.S. The mound lies at a distance of 0.2 km to the east of village. The area of the mound is 6 acre. Height of the mound is 3 meter. *Paancho peer baba ka Sthan* is located on the mound. The ceramic industry found is LM.

Gulchappa: The village lies on latitude 81⁰39′ N and longitude 26⁰50′50″ E. It lies 10 km to the north-west of the P.S. The mound lies at a distance of 0.7 km to the south-west of village. The area of the mound is 12.8 acre. Height of the mound is 0.2 meter. *Phoolwari* is located on the mound. The ceramic industry found is LM.

Hayat Nagar (1): The village lies on latitude 81⁰46′ N and longitude 26⁰49′ E. It lies 8 km to the north of the P.S. The mound lies at a distance of 0.2 km to the west of village. The area of the mound is 0.4 acre. *Shiva Mandir* and *Prathmik Vidyalaya* are located on the mound. The ceramic industry found is LM.

Hayat Nagar (2): The village lies on latitude 81⁰46′ N and longitude 26⁰49′ E. It lies 10 km to the north from the P.S. The area of the mound is 10 acre. Height of the mound is 3.3 meter. Mound is called *Deeh*. The ceramic industry found is LM.

Jalalpur: The village lies on latitude 81⁰44′15″ N and longitude 26⁰46′40″ E. It lies 3 km to the north of the P.S. The area of the mound is 2 acre. *Lala Narottam Das's samadhi* is located on the mound. The ceramic industries found are OCP, NBP, G, EM and LM.

Kakrahiya: The village lies on latitude 81⁰43′15″ N and longitude 26⁰43′10″ E. It lies 6 km to the south of the P.S. The mound lies at a distance of 0.2 km to the south of village. The area of the mound is 6 acre. The ceramic industry found is LM.

Katra: The village lies on latitude 81⁰45′20″ N and longitude 26⁰50′40″ E. It lies 1.5 km to the north-east of the P.S. The mound lies to the north of the village. The area of the mound is 1 acre. Height of the mound is 3.3 meter. *Qila* and *Hanuman Mandir* are located near the mound. The ceramic industry found is LM.

Khairanpur: The village lies on latitude 81⁰45′20″ N and longitude 26⁰46′20″ E. It lies 2 km to the north of the P.S. The mound lies at a distance of 0.6 km to the west of *Sharda Sahayak* Canal. The area of the mound is 5 acre. Height of the mound is 3 meter. The bricks of sizes 10x6x2.5 and 6x5x3.5 inch are found on the mound. *Satya Sai Data ka Ashram* is located on the mound. The ceramic industry found is LM.

Kotara: The village lies on latitude 81^{0}45′20″ N and longitude 26^{0}50′40″ E. It lies 13 km to the north of the P.S. The mound lies to the south-west of the village. The area of the mound is 10 acre. Height of the mound is 3 meter. The bricks of sizes 10x6x2.5 and 7x6x2 inch are found on the mound. *Dihawa* and *Sare Shaheed Baba ka Sthan* are located on the mound. The ceramic industries found are EM and LM.

Laluapur: The village lies on latitude 81^{0}46′ N and longitude 26^{0}43′10″ E. It lies 3 km to the east of the P.S. The mound lies at a distance of 0.8 km to the south of village. The area of the mound is 16 acre. Height of the mound is 2.4 meter. The bricks of sizes 6x4x2 inch are found on the mound. *Adam Shah Baba ka sthan* is located on the mound. The ceramic industry found is LM.

Manapur: The village lies on latitude 81^{0}44′50″ N and longitude 26^{0}43′50″ E. It lies 3 km to the south of the P.S. The mound lies at a distance of 0.8 km to the north of village. The area of the mound is 4 acre. Height of the mound is 2.6 meter. *Suri Dheep Talaab* is located on the mound. The ceramic industries found are OCP, NBP, K, G and LM.

Mazaffarpur ka Purwa: The village lies on latitude 82^{0}47′40″ N and longitude 26^{0}46′40″ E. It lies 7 km to the north-east of the P.S. The area of the mound is 5 acre. Height of the mound is 1.5 meter. *Itiya Shaheed Baba ka Sthan* and a *Nala* are located on and near the mound respectively. The ceramic industries found are OCP and Middle Chalcolithic (of corded ware tradition).

Meenapur Fagauli (Thakuran Fagauli): The village lies on latitude 81^{0}43′30″ N and longitude 26^{0}49′30″ E. It lies 9 km to the north of the P.S. The mound lies at a distance of 0.4 km to the south of village. The area of the mound is 10 acre. Height of the mound is 4.5 meter. The bricks of sizes 8.5x6x2 and 9.5x5.5x2.5 inch are found on the mound. *Kothi Bhawani* is located on the mound. The ceramic industry found is LM.

Meerapur: The village lies on latitude 82^{0}44′30″ N and longitude 26^{0}49′40″ E. It lies 1.5 km to the south-east of the P.S. The area of the mound is 4 acre. Height of the mound is 2 meter. *Unche Baba ka Sthan* is located on the mound. The ceramic industry found is LM.

Muzaffarpur: The village lies on latitude 82^{0}47′40″ N and longitude 26^{0}46′40″ E. It lies 6 km to the north-east of the P.S. The mound lies at a distance of 0.5 km to the east of the village. The area of the mound is 10 acre. *Shaheed Baba ka Sthan* and *Deehawa* are located on the mound. The ceramic industry found is LM.

Pilkhawa: The village lies on latitude 82^0 N and longitude E. It lies 4 km to the north of the P.S. The area of the mound is 4 acre. Height of the mound is 2 meter. *Deehawa Hanuman Garhi* is located on the mound. The ceramic industries found are OCP, NBP and EM.

Pure Hussain Khan: The village lies on latitude 81^{0}45′40″ N and longitude 26^{0}45′20″ E. It lies 1 km to the east of the P.S. The mound lies to the north-east of the village. The area of the mound is 1 acre.

Height of the mound is 0.9 meter. *Devkali Mandir* and *Surhur Talaab* are located on and near the mound respectively. The ceramic industry found is LM.

Raheemganj Mela: The village lies on latitude 81^{0}46′10″ N and longitude 26^{0}48′50″ E. It lies 9 km to the south-west of the P.S. The area of the mound is 7 acre. Height of the mound is 3.3 meter. *Bheetawa* is located on the mound. The ceramic industries found are EM and LM.

Ram Sharan Daspur: The village lies on latitude 81^{0}49′15″ N and longitude 26^{0}49′50″ E. It lies 7 km to the west of the P.S. The mound lies to the east of the village. The area of the mound is 2 acre. Height of the mound is 1.5 meter. The bricks of sizes 8.5x5.5x3 inch are found on the mound. *Kot Talaab* is located near the mound. The ceramic industry found is LM.

Rauza Goan: The village lies on latitude 81^{0}42′45″ N and longitude 26^{0}47′30″ E. It lies 9 km to the north of the P.S. The area of the mound is 4.4 acre. Height of the mound is 1.6 meter. *Deehawar Baba ka Sthan* is located on the mound. The ceramic industries found are OCP and LM.

Rudauli Mohalla Pure Khan: The village lies on latitude 81^{0}45′20″ N and longitude 26^{0}45′20″ E. It lies to the north of the P.S. The mound lies at a distance of 0.3 km to the north of village. The area of the mound is 1.2 acre. Height of the mound is 1.8 meter. *Sheikh Safi's* shrine is located on the mound. The ceramic industry found is LM.

Rudauli: The village lies on latitude 81^{0}45′ N and longitude 26^{0}45′30″ E. It lies 1 km to the east of the P.S. The area of the mound is 1 acre. *Deokali Mandir* is located on the mound. The ceramic industry found is LM.

Sahini: The village lies on latitude 81^{0}43′ N and longitude 26^{0}48′10″ E. It lies 7 km to the north-west of the P.S. The mound lies at a distance of 0.4 km to the west of village. The area of the mound is 6 acre. Height of the mound is 1.5 meter. The bricks of sizes 9x6x2, 11x6x2 and 8x7x2 inch are found on the mound. *Bhilasiya* Lake is located near the mound. The ceramic industry found is LM.

Shatrughan ka Purwa: The village lies on latitude 81^{0}47′ N and longitude 26^{0}30′ E. It lies 5 km to the south-east of the P.S. The mound lies at a distance of 0.5 km to the north of village. The area of the mound is 3 acre. Height of the mound is 1.3 meter. A place called *Saraiya Bheet* is located near the mound. The ceramic industry found is LM.

Sohsa Mauja Sarai Mugal: The village lies on latitude 81^{0}47′40″ N and longitude 26^{0}44′ E. It lies 4 km to the east of the P.S. The mound lies at a distance of 0.3 km to the west of village. The area of the mound is 1 acre. Height of the mound is 0.9 meter. *Mundia Talaab* is located near the mound. The ceramic industry found is LM.

Tanda Khulasa: The village lies on latitude 81^{0}42′ N and longitude 26^{0}46′40″ E. It lies 5 km to the west of the P.S. The mound lies at a distance of 0.1 km to the south-west of village. The area of the mound is 8 acre. Height of the mound is 1.2 meter. *Akausa Talaab* is located near the mound. The ceramic industry found is LM.

Abbreviations:

B.S	-	Black Slipped
EM	-	Early Medieval
G	-	Gupta
K	-	Kushan
Km	-	Kilo Meter
LM	-	Late Medieval
NBP	-	Northern Black Polish Ware
OCP	-	Ochre Color Pottery
P.S.	-	Police Station
TC	-	Terracotta

References:

1. Kumar, V. 2018. *A Note on Chariot Burials found at Sanauli district Baghpat U.P.* Indian Journal of Archaeology. p. 748.
2. *Ibid.* p. 742.
3. Kumar, V. 2017. *Archaeological Gazetteer of Aligarh & Hathras Districts with special reference to OCP & Other Proto Historic Cultures of Indo-Gangetic Plains.* Indian Journal of Archaeology. pp. 89-94.
4. *Ibid.* pp. 95-98.
5. *Ibid.* pp. 100-101.
6. *Ibid.* pp. 203-226.
7. *Ibid.* pp. 236-237.
8. Kumar, V. 2018. *A Note on Chariot Burials found at Sanauli district Baghpat U.P.* Indian Journal of Archaeology. p. 736; Manjul, S.K. & A. Manjul. 2018. *Recent Excavation at Sanauli, District Bagpat, U.P: A Landmark of Indian Archaeology.* 'Puratattva, No. 48. Indian Archaeology Society, New Delhi'. pp. 220-225.
9. *Gazetteer of India Uttar Pradesh, Faizabad Part-I.* pp. 28-30.
10. *Ibid.* pp. 30-31.
11. *Ibid.* pp. 31-32.
12. *Ibid.* pp. 32-34.
13. *Ibid.* pp. 34-37.
14. *Ibid.* pp. 37-41.
15. *Ibid.* pp. 41-53.
16. *Ibid.* pp. 53-70.
17. *Ibid.* pp. 70-72.
18. Fuhrer, A. 1969. *The Monumental Antiquities and Inscriptions in the North-Western Provinces and Oudh.* "Archaeological Survey of India". Indological Book House, Varanasi, India. p. 301.
19. *Ibid.* p. 302.
20. *Ibid.* p. 301.
21. *Ibid.* p. 301.